CROWOOD COLLECTORS' SERIES

British Army Cap Badges of the Twentieth Century

CROWOOD COLLECTORS' SERIES

British Army Cap Badges of the Twentieth Century

ARTHUR WARD

THE CROWOOD PRESS

First published in 2007 by
The Crowood Press Ltd
Ramsbury, Marlborough
Wiltshire SN8 2HR

www.crowood.com

British Library Cataloguing-in-Publication Data
A catalogue record for this book is available from the British Library.

ISBN 978 1 86126 961 4

Photograph previous page: Cap badge of The Buffs (the Royal East Kent
Regiment).

Typeset and designed by
D & N Publishing
Lambourn Woodlands, Hungerford, Berkshire.

Printed and bound in India by Replika Press PVT. Ltd.

DEDICATION

To an 'Old Buff', 22820111 A.F. Ward.

Well Dad, painstakingly collecting all those badges down the years was worthwhile. It certainly helped me – they are the basis of the collection within this book. Where would I have been without them and your knowledgeable answers to my interminable telephone calls?

And to my Mother, for marrying someone with a love of the past and then passing the genes on to me – another armchair historian.

Arthur Ward (senior), then a sergeant in The Buffs (The Royal East Kent Regiment), with Jean Ward holding the author, apparently dressed for Arctic warfare.

ACKNOWLEDGEMENTS

Special thanks to my darling Tamara, to whom British Army cap badges occupy a distinct and special space in her psyche!

I cannot thank Richard Ingram enough for his unselfish willingness to come to the author's rescue when needed. Cheers, Dickie!

I would also like to thank the following for their kind help during the preparation of the book: Roy Smith, Barry Hardy (of American Patrol), Rod Flood (of Minden Militaria), Nick Hall, Arthur Frederick Ward and Chris Toft.

INTRODUCTION

Collecting military insignia – principally badges – has long been a popular pastime. Being robust in nature, army cap badges have generally survived in quantity and are still relatively accessible to the novice collector. However, prices continue to rise. Although they are a sound investment and form the basis of an interesting militaria collection, the enthusiast must know what to do to avoid wasting money on 'wrong-uns'.

Badges possess one virtue that has not much changed and is still of enormous appeal to the collector – they do not take up too much space and can be displayed or transported with ease. I intend to explain the best ways to exhibit, store or ship collections, large and small. However, as Kipling and King said in their classic, two-volume reference work, *Head-dress Badges of the British Army*, if you do start collecting badges you will soon get hooked: 'Once you decide to join the ranks of enthusiastic badge collectors, you are immediately in danger of contracting a "disease" which, although not fatal, may well become obsessional.'

Most badge collectors started as schoolboys, perhaps being given a handful of them belonging to a relative or being tempted by a glittering array of brass insignia in a tray on display at a nearby junk shop. The majority of these aficionados carried their passion into adulthood and, if they still collect today, have seen the value of their collections increase dramatically.

Although cap badges can no longer be picked up for a few pence, they are still affordable, and today, with the number and variety of units in the British Army shrinking as the Ministry of Defence endeavours to reap the savings afforded by the amalgamating of famous formations into 'super regiments', the supply of once familiar insignia is drying up, although individual cap badges may still be found at car boot sales, in charity shops and following a rummage among the bits and pieces accumulating in junk shops. So now is a great time to collect.

This book is not intended to compete with the famous works of Kipling and King or F. Wilkinson – their works are still the standards – rather it is intended to encourage novices to start collecting, to avoid the pitfalls and the fakes and re-strikes and to understand which badges are the most valuable. It will also explain where to find badges and tell the reader what to do in order to protect and display them when he has purchased them.

But how do novices begin to decipher the intricacies of regimental heraldry? Where can they discover what is worth collecting and what is best avoided? Where can they learn how to judge authenticity and tell real from repro? This new collector's guide to British Army cap badges will provide newcomers to the hobby with all the details they need to begin or expand a collection of twentieth-century badges. It will give collectors a greater appreciation of the system of regional bonds that have for centuries united British fighting men within a unique system of unit loyalties. British regimental insignia, like the colours of football strips, engender an *esprit de corps* that is the envy of other armies, and by tracing the births, amalgamations and, in some cases, deaths, of famous regiments, enthusiasts can chart the tactics and battles of units and arms of the service from before the 1914–18 war to the present conflicts in Afghanistan and Iraq.

Beginning with a survey of twentieth-century military insignia in general, the book will describe the enormous expansion in unit emblems during and immediately after the Great War, the development of mechanized units and air liaison branches and the rationalization of insignia designed to harmonize with the new Second World War battledress. It will also consider post-war developments in badges resulting from the amalgamations of the 1960s and the introduction of anodized Staybrite badges. Incidentally, even the palpably less impressive, anodized badges are becoming increasingly collectable now. Made from anodized aluminium, a by-product of Britain's vanished motor industry and consequently no longer manufactured here any more, as with all collectables, their value is governed by market forces and the increasing rarity is pushing prices upwards.

A favourite book into which I look from time to time admirably sums up the spirit of the British Army. In W.G. Clifford's *Peeps at the British Army* (A. & C. Black, 1915) the author has this to say:

> For some reason or other, possibly on account of our national temperament, the British soldier is singularly unresponsive to the appeals of eloquence, which is just as well, as the average British officer, although he can say a few words very much to the point on occasion, is not a conspicuous success when it comes to sustained flights of oratory. Thereby hangs a good story. During the Napoleonic wars a General commanding a British division, noticing that the French obtained splendid results by exhorting their men immediately before giving battle, issued an order that officers commanding regiments under him were to address their men on a similar plan. The order was not popular, but had to be obeyed, and this is how the tough old Colonel who had seen much war service obeyed it. He paraded his battalion, drew himself up proudly in front of his men, and said: 'The General's orders are that I am to address you to fill you with enthusiasm for the fight before us. You will now consider yourselves duly addressed and filled with enthusiasm accordingly.' No doubt the old Colonel understood his men, and every soldier knows that the 'no fuss' idea is as strong today as ever it was in our service. Perhaps we have gone too far in the direction of killing all show, especially since the universal introduction of khaki.

I am sure Mr Clifford would be dismayed at how the twenty-first-century Army is not only bereft of the 'show' and ceremony of the days of scarlet he lamented, but also because many of the regiments he would have been so familiar with are also long gone. However, I am equally sure that he would be heartened to see that, albeit in a greatly reduced form, the regimental structure he understood endures today and that the modern soldier abides by the 'no fuss' rule as much as his Edwardian predecessor ever did.

Naturally, the book will also consider recent developments in the badge-collecting trade, notably the development of the online market place and the significance of auction sites such as eBay.

This book is principally concerned with Army cap badges of the twentieth century. Fortunately for the novice, there is a pretty simple way of determining which badges originate from the first half of the century, as opposed to those from the second: careful study of the crown surmounting the badge design, either the King's (Tudor) crowns or the Queen's (St Edward's crowns).

Queen Victoria reigned from 1837 until 1901 and was succeeded by her son Edward, who reigned as King Edward VII until 1910. So, apart from one year (1901), King's crowns embellished Army cap badges until the accession of Queen Elizabeth II in 1952, when they featured a Queen's crown again. They still do, and, at the time of writing (New Year's Day, 2007), it appears that they will continue to bear Her Majesty's mark for many years to come.

For the record, the lineage of twentieth-century British monarchs is as follows: Victoria (VR 1837–1901); Edward VII (EVIIR 1901–10); George V (GVR 1910–36); George VI (GVIR 1936–52); and Elizabeth II (EIIR) from 1952 until now. Collectors should note, however, that although Edward VIII, who succeeded George V in 1936, soon abdicated and was not crowned, some insignia bearing his cipher EVIIIR do exist.

MILITARY BADGES: A BRIEF HISTORY

In the Beginning

Since classical times, groups of opposing warriors have fought each other on the field of battle. It helped, of course, if rival belligerents could distinguish between their warriors and those of the enemy. It was equally important that a hierarchy of leadership could be seen clearly. Military costume and insignia were born.

The Assyrian army of the eighth century BC was not only the first army to be entirely armed with iron

The lure of a man in uniform has endured down the ages – witness this popular 1940s' song sheet.

weapons, in its time it was the largest ever seen and, comprising between 150,000 and 200,000 men, it was the first to require a systematic form of insignia. The Persian, the Macedonian, the Greek and the Roman armies that followed were larger and required even more organization. Indeed, the modern word 'insignia' is derived from *signa* – the Latin for 'standard'. Roman standards or *signa* were the tall, decorated poles topped with imperial eagles, which each century, cohort or legion within the army rallied around and protected to the death.

However, even the army of ancient Rome, whose legions comprised the first regular troops who undertook regular tours of operational duty overseas, was standardized only to a point: long-serving centurions wore breast-plates embossed with ornamental designs, which, in some ways, correspond to modern length of service or campaign insignia.

For long after the fall of Rome, most nation states depended for their defence on hastily raising troops from the body public, arming and equipping them with whatever was at hand and individuals wore their own clothes.

The feudal system in Western Europe saw the first real attempts to regulate matters. Heraldic devices adorned shields, tabards and banners, identifying individual allegiance to a lord or master. At around this time the most important form of battlefield emblem was the standard or ensign (derived from the French *enseigne* and the Latin plural *insignia*). The rank of 'ensign' denoted a junior officer responsible for bearing this large and colourful flag. Being visible amid the smoke and confusion of combat, such flags were used as rallying points around which rival forces could assemble. They literally followed the colours.

In Britain, the first systematic use of 'insignia' that could identify individual units, began in Cromwell's time. Regulation was the order of the day in the New Model Army and soldiers wore fairly regular dress and could expect fairly regular pay. Although mostly garbed in the ubiquitous lobster pot helmet and buff coatee, these soldiers experienced the first real military segmentation, in terms of rank and arm-of-service, which continues to this day and has contributed to the unique *esprit de corps* for which the British Army is famous. But despite this attempt at standardization, rival armies on Civil War battlefields were still quite difficult to distinguish. It was not until 1660, eleven years after the war ended, that the restoration of Charles II saw the creation of a regular standing army. But, even then, commanding officers enjoyed great licence as to how they dressed and equipped their soldiers and battlefield formations could present a hotchpotch of uniforms and equipment.

The Introduction of System

The Duke of Cumberland's reforms in 1747 introduced a regular system of numbering for individual regiments, indicating their precedence. In 1751 a Royal warrant first introduced the term 'badge' for metal insignia initially appearing on leather cartridges. A clothing warrant of 1768 regularized the positioning of metal badges for grenadiers on their bearskin caps.

Insignia in the modern sense were not fully adopted by armies until well into the later half of the eighteenth century, although regiments began to be numbered from 1751, with these numbers appearing on buttons from 1767. At this time, the elaborate Tarletons and peaked turbans were adorned with metal badges identifying differing units. Shakos, tall cylindrical headdresses copied from the Austrians (who had copied the design from Hungarian Magyars), were introduced in 1800. These 8in-tall 'stovepipes' featured large plates depicting unit insignia and were adorned with plumes denoting regular, light or grenadier companies; they quickly replaced the surviving mitres and tricorns. Headdress was supplemented

by gorgets, a reminder of the days of armour. Officers wore these around the throat, denoting regiment and rank and indicating the fact that the wearer was on duty. It was not until 1830 that they ceased to be worn in the British Army. Pewter buttons featuring the numbers of individual regiments also acted as an indication of service. This period also saw the introduction of devices such as shoulder boards identifying rank. Previously status was identifiable only by the quality and the cut of the uniform or type and the prestige of the weapons borne, either of which would have identified officer rank.

By the nineteenth century everything had become systemized to the extent that the concept of individual units identified by name and number and individual soldiery by standardized emblems of rank and arm of services was internationally accepted.

Regional Linkages

However, the British Army was different from those of other nations in one important respect: after Edward Cardwell's reforms of 1868 Britain was the only country that had concentrated on establishing precise regional bonds (not merely numbers) within its soldiery. Consequently, elaborate heraldic provincial identities were adopted to denote regional loyalties. Most other countries organized their military units solely on the less emotive and rather more impersonal system of unit numbers.

The reforms of the Secretary of State for War Hugh Childers came into effect in 1881, when the numbering system for regiments was discontinued and county affiliations continued to be strengthened. Most of the single-battalion regiments were combined into two-battalion regiments with, for the most part, county names in their titles. This created a force of sixty-nine line infantry regiments, consisting of forty-eight English, ten Scottish, eight Irish and three Welsh regiments. The British soon discovered that fighting men fought with vigour if they were part of the 'Glosters', 'the Wessex Regiment' or 'the East Kents', and not simply identified as the 'the 4th Regiment of Infantry of the Line'.

RIGHT: **A scene typical in British streets in 1940. A Home Guard sergeant chats to a member of the women's Auxiliary Territorial Service (ATS), while, carrying his gas mask, a civilian stands on steps, painted with a white strip to prevent injury to pedestrians during the nightly blackout.**

BELOW: **Layout of British and Commonwealth badges including: bronze cap badges for officers: Queen's, Army Service Corps (of Great War vintage winning the 'Royal' prefix in 1921 and becoming the RASC); metal line infantry cap badges: Buffs, Royal Fusiliers, Suffolks, East Yorkshires, Black Watch, Volunteer Battalion Post Office Rifles; Second World War plastic economy badges: Royal Artillery (bomb), Royal Engineers, Durham Light Infantry, King's Royal Rifle Corps, Devonshire Regiment; corps badges: Royal Artillery, Royal Engineers, RASC, REME, ATS; foreign and Commonwealth: Australian Commonwealth Military Forces, Free Dutch Volunteers; miscellaneous: Royal Marine other ranks' helmet plate, RM other ranks' cap badge, RN officer's beret badge and badge of the Palestine Police.**

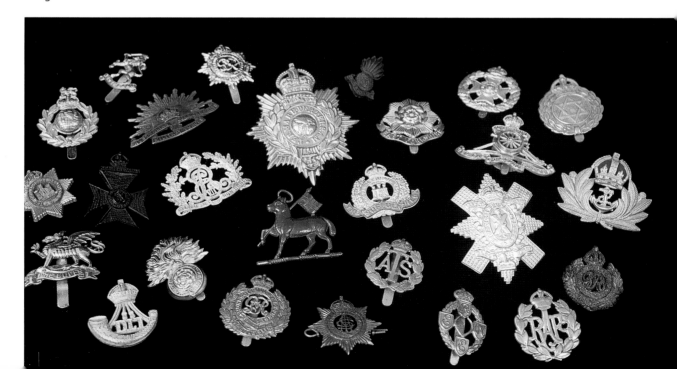

The 1880s also saw the British Army adopt cloth helmets, which remained in service until 1914. Because the older shako plates were unsuitable and the recent reforms had encouraged territorial titles to replace regimental numbers, new, eight-pointed helmet plates, the forerunners of twentieth-century cap badges, were designed for the new headgear.

It should be noted that, even as late as 1913, the Household Cavalry, for example, was distinguished by its uniform and was without a cap badge. However, the issue of khaki uniforms to the regiment in that year made the provision of badges a necessity and a bronze cap badge was issued.

Perhaps the most famous Secretary of State for War was Lord Haldane. His reforms of 1907–08 saw the creation of the Imperial General Staff under a senior officer who was its Chief. Under his direction, the Army also took stock of the changes forced upon it by the ascendancy on the battlefield of the quick-firing, bolt-action rifle, a revolutionary weapon. This combined with the use of camouflage and cover to enable 'fire and movement' and the influential tactics of Boer 'commandos' during the South African War of 1902 quickly encouraged the British to revise their service regulations. Even the wide-brimmed slouch hats worn by the Boers quickly found their place in British Army stores.

New Century, New Changes

However, the twentieth century was the harbinger of even newer techniques of warfare. The advent of mechanization, previously unimagined small arms accuracy and the need for increased stealth and concealment on the battlefield dictated further radical developments in dress and equipment.

The introduction of khaki uniforms and shrapnel helmets, which soldiers were forced to wear if they were to survive the explosive munitions showering them while sheltering in First World War trenches, necessitated the adoption on British uniforms of what were originally called 'battle patches'. With no insignia on helmets and shoulder titles being indistinguishable at a distance, these cloth devices readily identified battalions or brigades within a division. They thus enabled commanders to make battlefield dispositions without the need to be present among the front-line fighting. For the first time, senior officers could lead their men into battle from the secure locations far behind the front. Despite the somewhat pragmatic reason for their introduction, the adoption of such patches quickly engendered displays of unit loyalty and pride (the heroic activities of the 51st Highland Division, for example, spring to mind). Although introduced

Broad selection of British Second World War cloth insignia, including qualification, unit and field service emblems. Shown: parachute wings and 'parachute-trained' badge; tank crewman; machine gunner; motorcyclists; the crossed swords of a PTI (physical training Instructor); 5th AA Division; printed 43 Wessex flash; grey and yellow embroidered Army Catering Corps field service strip and a set of three embroidered, red, infantry seniority strips.

Second World War (King's crown) Australian and Commonwealth military forces' cap badge (General Service badge).

without much thought for the morale of the individual soldier, these patches went some way to ameliorating the depersonalization of trench warfare.

Ironically, although the British had long cherished distinct regimental individuality – difficult to express when soldiers were wearing plain steel helmets – the armies of Germany and France, which had long used a more impersonal system of numerical identification, found that their method worked well in the new battlefield conditions. Their uniforms sported clear unit numbers on tunic collars, supplemented by piping (*Waffenfarbe*) on collars and shoulder boards denoting arm of service. So, even in mud-splattered steel *Adrianne* (French) or *Stahlhelm* (German) headgear, French and German troops could more clearly exhibit their unit or arm-of-service identities.

At the end of the war in Britain it was decided that most of the enormous variety of insignia, some of it distinctly unofficial, that had crept back on to combat uniforms should be removed. The new British battledress pattern introduced in 1939 was designed with homogeneous simplicity in mind. This new uniform, inspired by both science fiction and the favoured choices of international tank crews, then seen as the dashing twentieth-century cavalry, consisted of a stylish blouson and pleated, baggy trousers and was designed to suit soldiers for the new technological

age. It was also considered an important aspect of field security that, if a soldier were captured, this new uniform, sporting no markings other than slip-on shoulder boards that could be easily removed, would not reveal his unit and consequently the dispositions of troops. Black or green buttons were also introduced to replace the previous polished brass ones.

First World War British other rank's soft trench cap badged to a gunner in the RFA. Introduced in late 1916, replacing the now impractical, stiff service cap that could not be easily stored nor carried when the recently introduced steel helmet was worn. This example is made of wool though there are other versions made of a more drill type of cloth.

Khaki Tam-O'-Shanter or Balmoral bonnet. Introduced in 1915 and worn by Scottish troops during and after both world wars, the example shown belonged to a Canadian Scottish unit, the Toronto Scottish. It is of Canadian manufacture. The badge backing is Athol grey (the kilt of the London Scottish – the British regiment affiliated to the Toronto Scottish). All Commonwealth Scottish units were allied to a parent Scottish regiment.

Front cover of Picture Post from 1941 showing Gen Giffard LeQuesne Martel ('Q Martel') clearly displaying his senior officer's badge of rank on his officer's service dress cap. General officers had crossed swords; field marshals had crossed batons. Although he started out in the Royal Engineers, Martel developed an interest in tanks during the First World War. After his return from Dunkirk (he was CO of the 50th Northumbrian Infantry Division, which was part of the BEF) he was put in charge of the Royal Armoured Corps.

But despite the designers' good intentions, by the end of 1940 the purpose and spirit of these new uniforms was somewhat undermined by the adoption of visible, coloured, field-service flashes. By 1941 this adornment had been augmented by the adoption of divisional and in some cases regimental flashes. This development further undermined the purpose of the uniform. Indeed, by the war's end soldiers wore a wide range of insignia. Far from presenting a clean and almost nondescript appearance, they were decorated like Christmas trees. Insignia denoting rank, regiment, division, trade and qualifications (often produced in regimental colours, for instance, black on green for rifle regiments and black on red for the King's Royal Rifle Corps) were supplemented by war service chevrons, campaign ribbons and, in some cases, even regimental lanyards. The designers of the new, futuristically streamlined battledress could only weep.

Twentieth-century wars also encouraged the development of often quite small units, now collectively known as Special Forces. These adopted specific cloth insignia to describe their role or capability. These units naturally depended on being able to distinguish themselves from the rank and file. They were the elite. In the British Army the most famous units of this type included the Special Air Service (SAS), the Long Range Desert Group (LRDG) and the Special Boat Squadron (SBS).

ABOVE RIGHT: This Sussex Home Guard wears a Royal Sussex cap badge (his county regiment) on his khaki field service cap. A Home Guard shoulder title can just be seen, but his battalion number just below this is obscured. He is armed with a P17 rifle of US First World War vintage.

BELOW RIGHT: British Second World War vintage side caps: a glengarry of the Seaforth Highlanders worn by both British and Commonwealth associated Scottish units – this pattern being the most typical with its red, white and green dicing; Officers' field service cap in quality barathea cloth – a privately purchased item with both bronzed regimental insignia (Royal Artillery) and buttons; RAF ordinary airman's field service cap and brass badge introduced just before the war, replacing the previous stiff service cap with patent leather peak.

Germany

Nazi Germany burst upon the world stage in January 1933, with the choice of Adolf Hitler as chancellor – his party having gained the largest share but not the majority vote in the 1932 general election. Nevertheless, it did not take Hitler long to assume full power and to change things in an effort to consolidate power. One of the ways in which he did this was to stamp his authority over the armed forces, both by patronage – equipping the air force and the navy in direct contravention of the Versailles agreement – and by adorning each service arm with radically new uniforms and regalia. Nazi reforms were wholesale, uniforms, equipment and regalia were all designed from scratch. The Führer's favourite iconography had its roots in an imagined Teutonic past of Aryan supremacy and knightly chivalry and the emblems of his army were designed to echo this. Third Reich insignia united political, police and paramilitary organizations under the auspices of the Nazi Party. Consequently, there were many badges and emblems available – one reason why such insignia are still so collectable.

The other reason for the popularity of Third Reich badges is their undeniable quality. Though many are of dubious provenance there is no denying their visual excellence. Although many established military artists and designers were involved in the creation of the new insignia, chief among them was the Berlin-based artist and graphic designer Egon Jantke, who designed badges, medals and many Third Reich uniforms.

Design was one thing but manufacturing quality is another reason for their popularity and durability. It is worth mentioning the names of the two most important manufacturers: the Wuppertal-based Bandfabrik Ewald Vorsteher in particular, a name usually reduced to the acronym BeVo, is often featured on a badge's description; the other big manufacturer was Assman & Sons, of Ludenscheid.

As was mentioned earlier, colour had become an increasingly important part of German insignia since the turn of the century: uniform piping denoting arm-

Despite the terror and slaughter with which they will forever be associated, the Third Reich's badges and insignia remain popular. This selection includes the following: tank crewman's skull cap badge, metal eagle/swastika shield and national colours shield for the Afrika Korps pith helmet, Feldgendarmerie (military police) gorget, RAD (Reichsarbeitsdienst – national labour service) brass door plaque, miniature booklet (Battle in the East), party armband and a rare standard top from a German infantry old comrades' flag (NSKOV).

of-service, party affiliation, rank hierarchy and level of responsibility; gold, for example, usually took precedence over silver.

Hitler also managed to combine the Nazi Party's official emblem, the swastika, with the traditional German eagle – effectively fusing the National Socialist German Workers Party (NSDAP) and the state. Consequently, individuals within the armed forces usually wore two principal badges, the Third Reich's interpretation of the national emblem – an eagle clutching a swastika in one of several shapes to depict army, air force or navy – and an organizational emblem to describe the arm-of-service. The badges and insignia of the German armed forces were a radical change from tradition and strikingly different from those used by other nations. Indeed, so eye-catching and imaginative were they that, forgetting the often-warped policies their wearers were ordered to pursue, collectors prize them above all others.

The USA

Together with British and Third Reich badges, the other big area for collectors comprises the badges and insignia of the United States. Twentieth-century American badges can trace their development back to the introduction of forage caps in the army in the nineteenth century. However, in 1902 the US Army introduced a new pattern of dress cap with a badge fixed to the front of the crown. Although initially produced in blue, in keeping with international practices, this hat was soon manufactured in khaki, with the blue service uniform being restricted to dress uniform purposes. The pattern of this cap is similar to that worn by American troops today.

Between 1911 and 1941 the US Army wore another distinctive type of hat, which sported the unit's badge. This was the classic 'Montana peak', a type still worn by some organizations today – most notably the Royal Canadian Mounted Police.

There are two other iconic US Army hats of the twentieth century. First, the 'Garrison' cap, a development of the American Great War 'Overseas' cap, which featured

rank insignia and coloured piping to denote arm-of-service (for instance, red and white for engineers). The second is the M1951 'Ridgeway' Field Cap, a development of the M1943 Field Service Cap but stiffened up by the addition of cardboard inserts to smarten the US Army up during the Korean War (rear echelons being seen to adopt a sloppy 'field garrison' appearance as in the television show *M.A.S.H.*). A development of this classic headgear was immortalized when it appeared with first-generation GI-Joe and Action Man figures.

The US Army was the fastest to move away from metal cap badges, which were usually national and collar insignia, which generally denoted unit affiliations, adopting instead a plethora of cloth patches to indicate the numerous units in the huge army. Simplicity is the key with all American heraldic devices and the designs of US Army patches, for example, are testament to the enduring skills of their creators. What could be simpler

Territorial Army (TA) recruiting leaflet from the 1950s.

and more recognizable than the patch of the US 1st Infantry Division: a red numeral one embroidered on an olive drab, irregular, shield shape, or that of the 1st US Army: a block capital black 'A' set on a divided white and red rectangle, or even the US Army Engineers: a white castle on a red ground?

Back to the object of this book: as the reader will see, even during the relatively short period of a century there is an enormous range of designs to collect. Together with a vast variety of designs there are also many different materials. Principally, of course, cap badges are manufactured from metal, but in times of shortage synthetic materials or cheap, one-piece, metal pressings were employed as replacement. Ironically, because of the changing security climate and because we live in a world where everyone – especially civil servants and legislative administrators – is more accountable, the days when surplus army badges found their way easily into the collectors' market have long gone. Today everything is accounted for and, if surplus, disposed of in secure conditions, it being considered too risky to let official emblems to fall into the hands of those with nefarious intent. Consequently, the badges of some of the newer British regiments are harder to find than those worn by formations on the Somme in 1916.

US Insignia: cloth 17th Airborne Division (Rhine Crossing); 6th Armoured Division (both of US manufacture); 9th Infantry Division (served in Europe and probably made in the UK); late war corporals' stripe worn both on field and class 'A' uniforms; group of three overseas service bars, each representing a year's service; second lieutenant (brass) and captain's (silver) bars (typical of the period with long bar pins for attachment to uniforms rather than the later short pins and clutch covers); enlisted soldiers' collar disc for medical branch (example shown is of late war manufacture with short pin and clutch cover attachment; frosted gilt officer's service cap badge (unusual, being produced in the UK by J.R. Gaunt).

BADGE COLLECTING: WHERE TO START

In the spring of 2006 an article in *Newsweek* was entitled 'Memorabilia from the Napoleonic Wars 200 years ago is attracting investors' attention'. Brian Charman, who runs the York-based antique militaria dealership Premier Emperor, was quoted as saying that, until recently, a commemorative Battle of Waterloo medal would have cost in the region of £150; 'today you could expect to pay £3,000.'

Far from being in decline, badge collecting remains big business. Although nineteenth-century items such as the Waterloo Medal will always command a high price, Army badges from the last century continue to increase in value. But buying the real thing and avoiding fake badges or those compromised by fraudulent alteration is the only way ever to build a collection of any value, however. Incidentally, the reader may be interested to learn that, following Waterloo, there was a great public desire to commemorate and celebrate the regiments involved in the campaigns against Bonaparte. Amazingly, as long ago as the 1820s an enterprise was established near Portsmouth to manufacture helmet plates for sale to collectors. So fake badges have been in circulation for a long time and to avoid purchasing facsimile badges requires preparation and forethought. The collector must know his beans and, in truth, a credible and satisfying collection can be achieved only if the collector follows a plan.

Self-adhesive Queen's Regiment badge in metallic finish. Dating from the early 1970s, this emblem was applied to vehicles such as Land Rovers.

Where to Start

The collector of British Army cap badges has such a wide variety to choose from that badge collecting certainly benefits from a systematic approach; but to build a planned collection is not a dull task, it provides focus and promises achievable goals, enabling the collector to maximize the potential of every purchase to gather a valuable and cohesive set of insignia based on a thematic approach. And what a variety of themes the collector has to choose from – there is such an

assortment of badges to choose from, even if the collection is restricted to only the twentieth century, that years can be spent amassing only a small proportion of what is available.

The more affluent collector might start with the large and elaborate blue cloth helmet plates worn by soldiers at the dawn of the twentieth century and a direct link to the even larger shako plates worn by troops for much of the nineteenth. The design of these

LEFT: **Coldstream Guards other ranks' puggaree badge.**

BELOW: **Set of British Army campaign, general service, long service and good conduct medals belonging to an RSM of The Queen's Regiment. These medals date from the late 1970s when the long service medal was issued for a minimum of 18 years' consecutive service. The medal on the far left was issued for service during the Mau Mau insurgency of the 1950s and the Arabian Peninsular medal is for service during the Aden emergency.**

plates tended to be more round than the old, rectangular plates worn on stove-pipe or Belgic shakos and the similar designs of headdress that continued up to the 1880s. They were generally based on an eight-pointed star design and featured removable centres denoting individual regiments.

Naturally, the first badges one thinks of are regimental cap badges, which were a direct descendant of the blue cloth helmet plates, the majority of which continued to be worn well into the 1960s. Then there are the badges of the numerous volunteer twentieth-century yeomanry regiments, created during the South African War and a valuable source of recruits during the two world wars. There are the badges of cavalry regiments to collect, and the enthusiast can follow their dismounted progression into today's Royal Armoured Corps. Then there are the badges of the numerous corps themselves and the individual variations of the badges of some of the reserve units affiliated to these corps, and finally, there are the badges that resulted from the many post-Second World War amalgamations. In 1994, Frederick Wilkinson, the eminent collector and authority on British Army badges said that for anyone looking for a collecting hobby that was 'well within the orbit of the collector with limited funds, then badge collecting still has much to offer'. Fortunately, more than a decade later and well into a new century, it still does. Furthermore, with the myriad amalgamations and the government's so-called 'streamlining' programmes, intended to increase the efficiency of the Army while reducing its cost, there are even more badges to collect.

Following even the apparently savage restructuring of the current *Strategic Defence Review*, announced in 2004 and due for completion in 2008, especially its main feature, the Future Infantry Structure, which called for the consolidation of all single-battalion infantry regiments other than the Guards into large regiments, the resulting Army will still be a large and complex animal.

In the British Army, above any other unit or formation, the regiment embodies the spirit of tradition, pride and *esprit de corps* that has made soldiers from the United Kingdom some of the most internationally respected fighting men on the battlefield. 'Pride in the

regiment' and an awareness of the many heroic actions of the men who have previously served with the colours act as an encouragement to every man who joins one. The weight of history, the sacrifices that earned battle honours, awards for gallantry or the legendary status simply acquired by an individual, who, faced with overwhelming odds fought and died doing his duty, are part of the rich fabric of every regiment. Recruits are soon imbued with the spirit of their own regiment and, though their loyalty is technically to monarch and country, their real allegiance is to the regiment and most are prepared to sacrifice anything for it. The Army cap badge, among all other emblems, identifies the individual regiment. Though it does not have the mystical significance of a regiment's colours, to lose a cap badge does not have the dread connotations which losing the colours has, it is a most important emblem.

Traditionally, a regiment numbered around 650 men. Many large regiments are divided into smaller units – battalions – and each of these would number around 650 men too. Battalions are sequentially numbered and are effectively 'mini' regiments in their own right, being composed of identical company structures, with their own logistical support and headquarters command and control.

I hope that this summary provides a good idea of the huge choice before the collector, but how does he go about tackling such a large and varied subject? One of the most common routes to starting a badge collection is found by accident, perhaps by the discovery of a small quantity of badges belonging to a relative. When one considers that in almost every British family grandfathers, great-grandfathers and uncles almost certainly spent some time in the military, either during one of the world wars or during the National Service which followed and existed between 1949 and 1960, this is hardly surprising.

Nick Hall, a long-time militaria collector and the owner of Southsea's famous Sabre Sales agreed: 'The first place where you should always start is with grandma and grandpa', he said, 'this is very important – what your grandma and grandpa did. Grandma, especially, should get credit for what she did. Indeed, currently there is an awful lot of interest in the collecting community about what the ladies did. Whether they were involved with nursing, worked on the land or in war production.'

The author can testify that, following his own recent online sale of civil defence items including uniforms, accessories and particularly badges belonging to members of the ATS (Auxiliary Territorial Service), FANY (First Aid Nursing Yeomanry) and WRVS (Women's Royal Voluntary Service), there is an enormous interest in so-called 'home front' items. With the subject now being part of the National Curriculum, even in the early Key Stages, those involved in 'living history' outreach programmes in primary and secondary schools have generated a great demand for previously overlooked items.

Sources of Information

So, other than with items inherited from family members, how should the novice collector begin? Not surprisingly, the first step towards understanding the variations in the design and finish of the many badges available requires research. Perhaps the best way to get an overview of the range of badges in existence is to visit a museum, and the national collections provide

the best way to do this, beginning with the National Army Museum in London. This superb institution covers the development of the Army as back as far as 1066 and its Uniforms, Badges and Medals Department contains over 250,000 badges and 20,000 medals, including thirty-seven Victoria Crosses. Obviously not all of these are on show, but many fine examples of twentieth-century badges may be viewed in the World Wars Gallery, covering the period 1905–45 and in the Fighting for Peace Gallery, which continues the story and covers the period 1946–2006.

Those collectors wanting to undertake a more in-depth study of regimental histories and the development of badges and other insignia can also make an appointment to visit the Museum's newly opened Templer Study Centre. This facility accommodates up to fifteen readers and offers access to the Museum's extensive archive. If a visit to London is not feasible the Museum is currently developing an extensive online archive of records and images, enabling the enthusiast to examine the collections via a personal computer.

Other valuable national collections include: the Imperial War Museum (which manages several sites in England, the most useful of which to the badge collector are at Lambeth and Duxford); the Museum of

Formed in 1956 when the Trucial Oman Levies (TOL) were renamed, these are badges of the Trucial Oman Scouts (TOS). The TOS were raised to provide escorts for junior British diplomats, known as political agents, who were deployed to administer British possessions in the Arabian Gulf. Shown adjacent to a TOS miniature flag are officers' and soldiers' silver badges, brass shoulder titles and a metal belt buckle badge.

Army Flying (at Middle Wallop in Wiltshire); the Tank Museum (at Bovington Camp, Dorset, which houses the collections of the Royal Armoured Corps, the Royal Tank Regiment and the Tank Corps); Firepower (The Royal Artillery Museum at the Royal Arsenal at Woolwich in London); and the Tower Armouries (in London and Leeds).

North of the border, Edinburgh Castle is home to a dazzling display of historic military artefacts; with more than one million annual visitors it is the second most popular ancient monument in the country after the Tower of London. Edinburgh Castle is still a working military establishment, providing the headquarters of the Scottish Division and with a permanent military guard on its main gate.

The large national museum collections might be the jewels in the crown as far as the display and conservation of military artefacts are concerned, but, for the badge collector, there are also other, smaller, regimental museum collections, which are often more specifically focused on individual units.

Although always rather small, in peacetime at least, the British Army has been such an integral part of the life of these islands and its regimental system such a crucial motivator of soldiery that, over the last century,

the country has acquired a rich collection of provincial regimental museums.

It is beyond the scope of this work to go into too much detail about individual museums – a good place to find out more about them is a search of the Army's own website (www.army.mod.uk/museums) – but it is worth looking at one or two to give the reader some idea of what is available and how to view their often unique collections of badges and associated militaria.

First and foremost it should be pointed out that the volunteers who mostly staff these museums are often ex-soldiers. These veterans, the custodians of their regimental histories and traditions, are generally able to explain the changes in badge development better than a recent graduate in curatorial processes or museum management could ever manage.

In England, the regimental museums include those of the Adjutant General's Corps (Peninsular Barracks, Winchester), The Airborne Forces Museum (Browning Barracks, Aldershot), The Buffs, Royal East Kent Regimental Museum Collection (Royal Museum and Art Gallery, Canterbury), Durham Light Infantry Museum Collection (Durham Art Gallery, Durham City), The Guards Museum (Wellington Barracks, London), The Honourable Artillery Company Museum (Armoury House,

Embroidered British Army badges of rank. Regimental quartermaster corporal and farrier quarter-master corporal, Household Cavalry (top left), post-Second World War line infantry WO 1 RSM (right), infantry staff sergeant's rank crown to be worn above stripes.

London), Manchester Regimental Museum (The Town Hall, Ashton-Under-Lyne), Oxfordshire & Buckinghamshire Light Infantry Museum (Slade Park TA Barracks, Oxford), The Queen's Own Hussars Museum (Lord Leycester Hospital, Warwick), Royal Regiment of Fusiliers (London) Museum (HM Tower of London) and the Worcestershire Yeomanry Museum (City Museum and Art Gallery, Worcester). This is just a selection, there are many more.

With its rich heritage of famous Highland and Lowland regiments, Scotland naturally also has its share of excellent regimental museums. The following are worthy of close inspection by the badge collector: The Argyll & Sutherland Highlanders Regimental Museum (The Castle, Stirling), The Black Watch Regimental Museum (Balhousie Castle, Perthshire), The Gordon Highlanders Museum (St Luke's, Aberdeen), The King's

Britain's Modern Army sold widely in 1943.

Own Scottish Borderers Regimental Museum (The Barracks, Berwick-Upon-Tweed) and the Royal Highland Fusiliers Museum (Sauchiehall Street, Glasgow).

In Wales, among others, the Royal Welch Fusiliers Museum (The Castle, Caernarfon), The Pembroke Yeomanry Collection (Scolton Manor Museum, Haverfordwest) and the Camarthen Militia and Volunteers Collection (Camarthenshire County Museum, Camarthen) are well worth a visit.

No visit to Northern Ireland by the serious collector could be complete without scheduling a trip to the Royal Inniskilling Fusiliers Regimental Museum (Enniskillen Castle, County Fermanagh). While there, the Royal Irish Regiment Museum at St Patrick's Barracks in Ballymena would equally repay a visit.

With experience, the collector will soon discover the enormous number of badge variants resulting from the developments in the yeomanry battalions early in the twentieth century. Regimental museums are a good place to see these and to study their individual peculiarities. They are also useful in enabling the collector to see exactly how badges were worn in service, most reference books merely showing a badge in isolation without the context of the particular headdress to which it was attached.

Provincial regimental museums are essential for the serious badge collector and there are plenty of them; by the time of writing the author had identified around 150 in the United Kingdom.

The other obvious source of information comprises reference books. The bibliography at the back of this book lists some of the best available. However, it should be noted that even the most comprehensive, such as the classic, two-volume work by Kipling and King, has omissions. The subject of badge collecting is so vast that no single work can ever hope to show the diversity of dress, rank and production type of every available cap badge, let alone all the variants where the crown altered following successive coronations.

Badges are an important part of Sabre Sales business. Nick Hall started collecting badges as a sideline; initially, he amassed a variety of swords, buying them for the equivalent of only 25p. Mind you, as the reader will glean from the photographs of 'the Legendary Nick Hall' in this book, he is rather old!

British Army post-Second World War RSM's rank armband to be worn around the wrist when in shirt-sleeve order.

Accurate research material is important to Nick; when he began collecting badges there were few reference books available and he had to teach himself everything from scratch.

> In those days there were very few books about militaria and no books about cap badges at all. It wasn't until later that people wrote books about them. Guido Rosignoli was one of the first people to write a book about cap badges and, as he lived quite near my home, he would come down and look through whatever badges I had.

Most enthusiasts will be familiar with the name Rosignoli, the author of numerous books about badges and often partnered by another familiar name, Terence Wise. Hall was fortunate to enjoy the association with such a scholarly expert.

I remember my father, an ex-regular who joined his father's regiment, The Buffs, in the early 1950s delving into his battered volume of Kipling and King's *Head-Dress Badges of the British Army* when he was actively collecting in the 1960s. I recall that he rarely made a purchase without checking this work for confirmation of the style and finish of an alleged collectable.

Another good source of information is dealers' catalogues. Due to the growth in business online these are not as numerous as they once were, but because of the peculiar demographics of badge collecting – a hobby with many participators perhaps too old or unwilling to invest in modern information technology – many established dealers persist in publishing illustrated catalogues to support their commercial activities. Thus the dealers' catalogues, with the often lavishly produced catalogues published before specialist sales by auction houses such as Wallis and Wallis, Bonhams and Sotheby's, along with those of specialists such as Bosleys (more of them later), are together an excellent (and cheap) way of finding out more about particular badges.

There is, however, another most useful resource open to most collectors and that is, of course, the internet. Simply by typing a regimental title into a search engine such as Google, the enthusiasts will almost instantly be confronted by a wealth of information. In the early days of the world-wide-web much of what was available was put online by fans desperate to be published in any form. Not surprisingly, much of what was thus made available was of spurious accuracy and provenance. While the web is still fortunately largely unrestricted and not subject to government interference nor editorial supervision, it has to be said that things have greatly improved as far as the variety and accuracy of online information is concerned. This is partly due to a kind of natural selection that has resulted in the most used sites getting ranked higher and higher in search engine listings. It stands to reason that the most visited sites must be providing a service to visitors, so this self-levelling league table seems to work.

The other great advantage with the internet is the facility it provides for enthusiasts to copy the photographs shown in individual web sites or in online auction listings. This provides another useful resource to the collector. But the final, and perhaps most obvious way the internet can be of use, is simply as a market place featuring thousands of items for sale. So, after entering a regimental title and the word 'badge', although the collector will be directed to several government-sponsored or veterans' association web sites, dozens of sale items for the badge in question will also pop up. The biggest is, of course, eBay and, regardless of any intent to purchase, the examination of badge listings can reveal much valuable information, often posted there for all to see, by knowledgeable enthusiasts.

Three Personal Experiences

To help you to decide how to approach the building of a themed collection, I thought it a good idea to gather the views of some individuals united by a common interest and involvement with British Army cap badges. Discovering how these collectors built their collections, the first for pleasure and the second for business, provides an interesting insight into the motivation and activities of the collector.

The first case study concerns my father. A long-service, regular soldier, he wore British Army cap badges for most of his career. In fact, nearly all the badges illustrated here were collected by him during the 1960s and the early 1970s. This is his story.

My interest in cap badges began almost as soon as I joined up. I joined the regular Army in August 1952 after leaving school the month before. While at school I had been in the Combined Cadet Force (CCF) in which I had reached the rank of cadet sergeant major.

I suppose my interest in the Army was fostered from early on in life. My father was a regular soldier serving in the Buffs, the Royal East Kent Regiment. I was born in Maymo, Burma, in 1934 while my father's battalion was on active service there.

I enlisted in the Buffs easily enough, having the right to do so because it was my father's old regiment and he had died a Buff in 1940, following his recall to the colours the previous year. My father had been caught up in the Dunkirk fiasco – actually being evacuated from St. Nazaire. At the age of six I still remember him coming home, carrying his rifle. He was soon posted to Devon where he was killed – blown up by a British mine because, as my mother always claimed, some 'idiotic Rupert of an officer' ordered him to collect firewood from a beach that was apparently mined as an anti-invasion preparation.

On enlistment in the regular Army I was posted to do my basic training at the Buffs' regimental depot – the 'new infantry barracks' in Canterbury, Kent, one of the most modern barracks built as recently as the 1930s.

The distinctive badge of a Royal Tank Corps crewman can just be seen on his beret. British Vickers Light Tanks like this never had to come face to face with German Panzers.

My keen interest in badge collecting really began in the 1960s. Although I liked the design of many of the badges belonging to Scottish regiments in particular,

I have to admit to being biased towards the design of the Buffs' badge. I thought the Buffs' dragon, awarded to the regiment by Queen Anne in 1707 in honour of their Tudor origins – a rare distinction – was, and still is, most striking. This motif is now embedded in the badge of the Princess of Wales's Royal Regiment (PWRR), but for me it harks back to 1572 when Queen Elizabeth I reviewed the Trained Bands of London. Because, the Buffs, the 3rd of Foot and The Queen's Royal Regiment, the 2nd of Foot are constituents of the PWRR the regiment is the senior regiment of line in the Army.

I remember that some soldiers used to collect badges and put them on their leather belts and the like – much like Steptoe's son Albert did in the famous TV sit-com. In my Army days there was pride in keeping badges, buttons, shoulder titles, collar dogs, belt brasses and the brass fittings on webbing as highly polished as possible. In fact, with all the corporals, sergeants and company sergeant majors about, not to do so was akin to committing suicide. And woe betide you if you came to the attention of the worst ogre of all – the eagle-eyed regimental sergeant major!

To be honest, I did not find such work a chore and throughout my training I got real satisfaction from going out on parade without ever being berated for

ABOVE: **Throughout the war His Majesty's Stationery office (HMSO) produced regular booklets documenting the activities of all those involved in the services or on the home front. This one looked at the British Army.**

RIGHT: **British Army sergeant's service dress rank insignia.**

having dirty brasses. However, to ensure that things were just right required the proper use of the 'button stick' to be certain that none of the polish used on the badges marked the uniforms to which they were sewn. My preferred method for polishing badges was to put Bluebell polish on to a piece of cardboard and buff the badge against this, being careful to ensure that fine details such as the regimental title weren't rubbed away. Of course, you would also have to clean the reverse of the badge, finishing off with a cloth.

Coming into contact with so many other regiments during my service career made me appreciate the diversity and, dare I say it, the beauty of a lot of cap badges. Like me, most serving personnel – including

National Servicemen – were reluctant to part with their badges. They embodied the pride of the regiment and for me and many other soldiers they were imbued with a value that is hard for anyone who hasn't been in the Army to understand.

In the early days of my collecting activities badges were fairly easily to find. The junk shops or antique shops of most towns, especially those with close regimental associations, usually sold Army badges. In those days cap badges could be bought for a very reasonable sum – usually between £1.00 and £1.50. Among the hardest badges to collect were those belonging to regiments not associated with your local area. I served in the Buffs so it was pretty easy to find their badges in shops throughout the home counties. However, it was much more difficult to find Scottish or Irish regimental badges on sale in southern England. Consequently, one had to resort to dealers and in those days that meant sending off for a thick, photocopied list of typewritten descriptions. Seldom did the collector have the luxury of seeing a photograph of the badge he wished to purchase. Today's collectors who can view colour images from the comfort of a desktop PC don't realize how lucky they are!

I began my collection with a full set of badges of the home counties regiments, The Buffs, the Middlesex Regiment, Royal Fusiliers, Royal East Surrey Regiment, The Queen's Royal Regiment, the Royal Sussex and the Royal West Kent Regiment When this quest had been completed I spread my net further and began

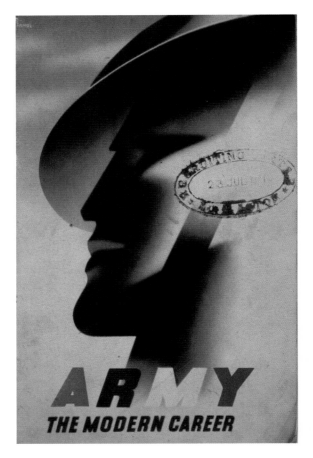

Strictly on message and in keeping with the suggestion that the Army was a truly modern career, this wartime recruiting leaflet employs the most contemporary graphic style available.

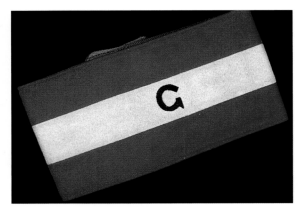

Second World War British General Staff Anti-Aircraft Command armband.

The author's father at the Tank Museum, Bovington, leaning on a Second World War Daimler armoured car. Behind him is a Sherman Firefly armed with a British 17pdr gun. It was really the only version of this ubiquitous tank capable of knocking out German Tigers and Panthers.

collecting more exotic badges – especially those belonging to Scottish regiments, which I had always admired. I was also particularly successful with my First World War collection, adding the Machine Gun Corps and the four badges of the Royal Naval Division (who served as infantry on the Western Front) to my growing collection.

One of the pleasures of collecting British Army badges is the evolving nature of regimental compositions – especially the frequent post-Second World War amalgamations. The Buffs were forced to amalgamate with The Queen's Own Royal West Kent Regiment and on 1 March 1961 became The Queen's Own Buffs Royal Kent Regiment (3rd, 50th and 97th of Foot) – for me, this was a most terrible occurrence. Worse was to come.

On 31 December 1966 yet another amalgamation took place and the Buffs became part of The Queen's Regiment, a hotchpotch of all the old home counties regiments, less the Royal Fusiliers who became part of the Fusilier Regiment. Like many of those involved with the amalgamations of the county regiments, I thought this was a complete disaster. Gone were the old county associations, lots of regimental pride and loyalty and, to my mind, they've never been since the amalgamation process began. But although the new badges were a patchwork of bits and pieces taken from the former cap badges and other insignia, such as the collar dogs, of the amalgamated regiments, they did provide more to collect!

In my opinion, though, 'modern', anodized badges, including Staybrite badges which no longer required polishing, present an artificial shine. Although far less elbow grease is needed to keep everything in order, I don't think that you can beat the polished finish of the old brass badges, collar dogs and buttons. From his days as a recruit a soldier soon gets into a routine of cleaning cap badges and other accoutrements – when I was a recruit, following the evening meal, there was a dedicated 'cleaning hour' every evening, Monday to Friday. During this time we cleaned our kit, 'Blancoed' our webbing and polished our boots and badges while being overseen by NCOs. Thank Heavens that cloth titles and other cloth badges were sewn on by the regimental tailors.

Today, badge collectors have to be especially careful to avoid damaged or fake items. One way to do so is to purchase items from reputable dealers. Many magazines, such as the Army's own periodical *Soldier*, feature advertisements from reliable merchants. One tip that can help to avoid buying a wrong 'un is to look at the reverse of a badge to see whether the impression is as clear as it would be if it had been officially struck. Collectors should also avoid badges where any repairs to the hasps or lugs are evident. Those badges that have perfectly flat backs, rather than the concave detail that results from a complex impression having being stamped through thin sheet metal, should also be avoided. The front of badge should obviously be clearly defined, with the regimental title clear and easy to read – of course, some allowance should be made for previous cleaning – but there's little value in an item with much of its detail rubbed away by years of vigorous bull.

So that's the ex-soldier's view. For the record, my father finished his Army career with the rank of regimental sergeant major (RSM). I wonder whether he remembered his days as a raw recruit each time he gave a poorly turned-out squaddie a dressing down …

By contrast there is the collector who becomes a dealer, a gamekeeper turned poacher, I suppose. Of course, to be commercially successful when trading in any area of collectables the individual has to forego any desire to covet things that might pass his way. They have a commercial value and must be sold for a profit to benefit the business. Although Nick Hall started collecting badges as a youngster, when he established Sabre Sales he had to become dispassionate about the objects that came his way. Starting a militaria business finished his collecting ambitions. He did not immediately become a militaria dealer. His first vocational choice was in estate agency. At the time, a period in the Territorial Army satiated his interest in all things military. When he left estate agency he joined the Bermuda Police.

'I got a kind of sub-job advising the Bermuda government on matters concerning militaria', he told me,

'I worked at Fort St Catherine and Gates Fort, both near St George, the old capital of Bermuda. Although that was 3,500 miles away, the knowledge I gained of the history of military matters while I was a schoolboy enabled me to catalogue the collection they had there.'

Hall was based in Bermuda from 1962 to 1969, where he met his wife. He told me that part of his job involved sorting out the many items that the Bermudan heritage department had bought cheaply ('You could buy a musket for £1.25') but about which they did not really know very much. 'They had acquired all this stuff but they didn't know what it was. It was just a great mishmash of things', he smiled.

I remember that in the Bermuda Police mess in Prospect, near Hamilton (Bermuda's capital), there was a wonderful board listing all the regiments that had served in Bermuda. This certainly whetted my appetite for badges and regalia.

In fact, Prospect Camp was the first military HQ in the territory so this collection of martial heritage is not surprising. 'It was a very good posting', he continued, 'because the government had to keep a garrison there because of the rumour that during the First World War a German U-boat landed a party ashore and actually posted a letter! Naturally, this was regarded as very bad form, so you would have lots of soldiers guarding Bermuda, which did have a very strategic purpose in the Second World War, with lots of infantry leaping about the place.'

Nick Hall, owner of Sabre Sales, seated in his spacious open-plan office.

Working with Nick Hall since he was knee high to a grass hopper, militaria supremo Rich ('Dickie') Ingram.

Upon his return to the United Kingdom Hall went into property development and rejoined the TA where he got a commission in the Royal Corps of Transport (RCT).

He set up Sabre Sales in 1987. The hobby he had loved as a youngster had changed radically. The prices for badges and Army surplus had risen dramatically, but were yet to reach the dizzying heights achieved later. 'You couldn't go out and pick up silver-inlaid Japanese matchlock rifles, for example, for small change anymore. I realized that I'd have to set up a business if I wanted to carry on', Nick recollected.

Soon after Sabre Sales was opened he approached Richard Ingram, who, though living in Scotland, was already well known as a most knowledgeable enthusiast, especially about aspects of British Army uniform development and particularly badges. Since its opening, Sabre Sales has expanded dramatically and now consists of three shops and two warehouses.

'Cap badges are still a big part of the business', Nick said, 'but it is completely different from what it was. In its early days the business sold original cap badges and they cost somewhere between 1s.6d and 7s.6d or 10s.'

Apparently, things changed when the market became flooded with repro items – not repro in the conventional

Like many, this Home Guard is a veteran of the Great War, as can be seen by his medal ribbons.

sense, but badges struck from the original dies that a competitor based in the Midlands had happened upon almost by accident. The dies were being disposed of because they featured the impressions of former regiments and were no longer required, being of scrap value for the metal content of their die-stamps. Realizing that he was on to a winner, this lucky individual, finding that he could not afford to carry home the entire haul, purchased those of the most obscure badges in the assembly; thereby ensuring he had the wherewithal to reproduce, from the original tools, some of the most rare and coveted badges. I shall discuss the confusing matter of such reproduction items struck from authentic dies in a later chapter.

The lot of the professional badge dealer has changed enormously in recent years. Hall told me that the days when film and television production companies employed militaria consultants on a full-time, salaried basis have long gone because these experts were costing too much. Nowadays, such companies will contact Hall and Sabre Sales direct, initially for free advice and then hope to reach agreement on the commercial hiring of uniforms and badges. Hall said that the immediate advice is always free because it involves three rather straightforward processes: 'First, a simple "Yes" or "No", I either have it or I don't,

secondly, what is practical – I might not have the quantity of authentic items available. The third stage involves finding a suitable alternative if that is acceptable. Often genuine items can't be used because they simply don't exist.'

Indeed, Hall told me that authentic US Second World War Pacific theatre uniforms were almost impossible to locate because, before returning from Guadalcanal or Tarawa, these soldiers were virtually in rags, their garments being burned before they disembarked. Japanese prisoners were forced to remove their uniforms, which were also burned, while they stood there naked so that if any grenades were concealed they were more obvious.

Like many of his professional contemporaries, Hall has witnessed a sea change in the militaria business in the last decade or so. As original items became scarcer, Sabre Sales has had to develop new, but related, income streams.

The enormous growth in re-enactment, with societies and living history groups appearing widely, has generated an enormous demand for repro militaria – uniforms, equipment and badges. Unlike twenty or so years ago, today it is now almost impossible to dress enthusiasts in authentic Second World War uniforms, for example. Uniforms of a similar cut or finish to original

Examples of military headdress piled high at Nick Hall's Sabre Sales.

A selection of British armed services caps and their badges at Sabre Sales.

items or complete repro ones are now sold or hired to satisfy demand. Consequently, post-war European army uniforms, cut to almost exactly the same patterns as the Second World War British or American originals and manufactured overseas for Empire and Commonwealth troops, are now employed as more than adequate replacements for the real thing.

Authentic militaria is still very much part of Sabre Sales' business, of course, but to remain at the top of his game, Hall has had to diversify. I asked him what were now the most collectable twentieth-century badges, what are British badge collectors looking for now?

He said at the moment they are looking for all the new regiments. The government has created a lot of these and their badges will have to be turned in when the individuals leave the services. When you consider that a lot of these badges relate to high security-type troops, the authorities are naturally strictly controlling the manufacture and subsequent possession of these badges. Because the government owns the badge dies for these formations and will not release them for commercial use, the emblems of Special Forces and special reconnaissance units, for example, will be difficult to obtain. However, the badges for the new super regiments will be easier to get hold of. They will become available because there will be a demand for them in the TA and Cadet Force and consequently these badges will be more liberally distributed.

Interestingly, Hall told me of an incident regarding the Royal Regiment of Scotland badges issued to TA units, which might suggests that even this previously guaranteed source of supply might dry up. He told me that recently the distribution of these coveted new badges had actually come to the attention of local security forces. Apparently, quite a few newly issued badges were finding their way on to the market because the soldiers to whom they had been issued professed to have lost them, when, in fact, they were selling them to dealers. Hall went on to tell me of a previous incident involving the then new, metal black Royal Marine Commando titles intended to be worn on jumper epaulettes. A fresh consignment of these had mysteriously found their way into militaria shops.

I asked him about the relative scarcity of badges from the older regiments, for example, the Buffs. He said, 'Ironically, the Buffs suffered because they were disbanded as a regiment before the government established a recycling programme. Now that the government has adopted recycling, every single product of a "secure" nature is sorted out and those badges and collar badges that can be disposed of are sold to the trade. When the Buffs ceased to be, there were several factors limiting the supply of their obsolete badges. First, there was a perceived security risk; secondly, there was no recycling in operation and, finally, if a government department were disposing of

high-value items such as tank engines to the trade they couldn't be bothered with cap badges and collar dogs, so old Buffs' badges were seldom sold in bulk.'

If there were no organized channels for the government to dispose of unwanted badges in the days when my father was a collector, I asked Hall why then did it appear that you could still find them quite easily?

'Well, first of all there weren't as many people around as you think there were', he answered. 'Nevertheless, those people that did have them for sale could have got them from places such as film studios. There were certain regiments who featured on film quite regularly. Ironically, one of them The Wessex Volunteers didn't actually exist in reality, but then, funnily enough, it actually came into existence when that title, The Wessex, was used for a territorial infantry battalion.'

LEFT: **This Army recruiting leaflet was placed in the hands of an eager recruit in Derby.**

BELOW: **One of the many badge drawers at Sabre Sales.**

A fascinating story illustrating one route to market of authentic, unissued, British Second World War Army badges dates from Hall's childhood. Apparently Freddie Owen, a dealer in Eton High Street, acquired a huge quantity of British and Commonwealth badges, Army and RAF, from the manufacturers, A.R. Fabb Bros Ltd, in nearby Maidenhead. Fabb's, a company specializing in gold wire embroidery, had moved from London following a direct hit that destroyed their premises during the 1940 Blitz. They also made masonic regalia as well as items for the British services. Some detail for the real enthusiast: when Fabb's was established in 1887 an RN cap badge incorporating much real gold wire cost the equivalent of 27p.

When Hall visited Owen's shop he saw on sale there numerous bags, all of a similar size, filled with a wide variety of the war surplus production from Fabb's factory. Although Owen had bought the emblems in individual lots, he would separate and distribute these among the assorted bags. 'You never knew what you were getting', said Hall. 'On a good day, contents worth £10, on a bad day ten times less.' He told me much later that the remaining stock from Owen's shop ended by being auctioned at Wallis & Wallis, achieving very high prices.

Hall told me that the prices of badges continued in an upward trend. He said that he was surprised, when considering that so few people of what he called the 'old brigade' were still around, the myriad dealers and collectors who used to inhabit the stalls of London's Portobello Road, 'if they are still collecting must by now be of an age when they have got the three different types of Army Catering Corps badge and they don't need another one. And with the Army Catering Corps now being amalgamated with the Royal Logistical Corps making life all that much simpler for the collector anyway. Because of the rising value of Army badges, Sabre Sales fights very hard to keep the prices down because we want the collectors to continue to collect. You don't get people coming in any more saying that they are looking for a rare horse pistol because the horse pistols are now so expensive that that's a very specialized market.'

This led him to mention the team of authors famous for perhaps the best reference works about cap badges ever published: Kipling and King. Like all badge collectors, Hall often resorted to the classic reference works of Arthur Kipling and Hugh King. In fact, Hall was a personal friend of the late Hugh King, who died in 2006.

In 1940, before he joined the RAF, King, the son of a Farnham hairdresser, had the rare distinction of being the first man to join the Surrey town's newly formed Local Defence Volunteers (LDV), the forerunner of the

In the Second World War Britain was able to call upon the huge manpower resources of an Empire that was at its height. Soon soldiers of every hue and accent were rallying in support of the Mother Country.

Home Guard. King went to the local grammar school, which suffered many casualties among his fellow class-mates who had also joined the RAF. 'At the end of the war he was very lucky to still be alive', said Hall, 'so, because several people asked him about wartime badges, I think he thought "Well, I might as well start collecting." This was a perfectly sensible thing to do then with badges being so cheap. Everyone was collecting them. That's how he started.'

'Hugh's co-author Arthur Kipling was a most interesting chap', Nick said. 'He worked at Gale & Polden [the famous publisher of military reference works founded in 1888 and taken over by Purnell in 1963 only to be finally incorporated into the new British Publishing Company in 1964, then the largest printing company in Europe] and created the original badge charts and all the charts describing British divisional insignia. He personally told me that he selected the majority of the patches shown on these famous badge, but then said to the girls in his office, "Which ones would you like to be put on the posters?", and the badges were partly selected by what appealed to the ladies rather than their rarity, scarcity or battle appeal.'

1940 Second World War Soldiers' Sailors' and Airmen's Families Association fund-raising poster showing the heads of the three services: Ironside (Army), Dudley-Pound (Navy) and Newall (RAF).

Hall went on to tell me that these charts were printed with a space in the middle of the design. Local breweries apparently bought advertising on them, had their logos placed in the middle and put up on the walls of the pubs, whereupon the pubs would collect the badges and put them on the walls.

It should be noted that, apart from the famous two-volume work, *Head-Dress Badges of the British Army*, written with Hugh King, Arthur L. Kipling worked on numerous other reference works for Gale & Polden. Among them he revised Maj T.J. Edwards's classic post-war work *Regimental Badges*.

Hall told me that, ironically, one of the most popular badges collected today is that of the Royal West Kent Regiment. Why? Because, it has enjoyed massive promotion on television for the last forty years as the cap badge of the fictional Walmington-on-Sea platoon in the BBC's classic Home Guard sitcom, *Dad's Army*.

Hall pointed out that, when you find an Army peaked cap with a cap badge attached, collectors should be aware that they were not necessarily ever one and the same. Service caps and badges are issued separately and similarly disposed of. 'If you get a peaked cap from the government and it is brand new in its box', he said, 'it will usually have only the cap buttons and chin strap attached – but often this might not be affixed because each element is the product of a separate manufacturer. When the caps are handed in at the end of their lives I would guess that only around

2 per cent of them will still have their cap badge attached and this is only because the badges are very tired and at the end of their lives.' Hall pointed out that the numerous caps – all with badges attached – in stock in his shop have had the correct badge selected by him or another of his specialist colleagues and then 'married' to make the correct combination.

I asked him what he predicted for the future of badge collecting in Britain. He said, 'The future will see various specialist dealers continuing to increase their international business. Stephen Bosley [of Bosleys of Marlow] has absolutely cornered the market. Although it's impossible to be sure about what's going to happen – as events occur – fashion and taste have changed. For example, following the terrible activities of Michael Ryan in Hungerford, few people want to wear combat jackets any more, for fear of being thought a nutter.'

Nick did say that, with the future of the armed forces being somewhat in a state of flux these days – the reduction in the type and number of regiments and, a matter close to his heart, the future of the three principal Naval Dockyards, a subject of active national debate at the time of writing – there may be a groundswell of sentimental interest in the many fine units that have gone or been amalgamated. On the other hand, all the radical changes could engender bitterness and consequent disinterest. Certainly the activities of our overstretched Army in Iraq and Afghanistan have meant that soldiers now appear on

Collecting Players' cigarette cards was another way youngsters got to learn all about insignia such as RAF squadron badges.

television more often than they have in recent years and this has encouraged curiosity about Army units and their histories.

Hall told me that there were still some badges he was trying to get his hands on. Ironically, these are not old or classic ones but brand new cap badges. 'I've had only one badge belonging to The Royal Regiment of Scotland so far', he said. 'I've seen them on parade at the Edinburgh Tattoo, so I know that they wear their original unit's badge on their collars, the Royal Scots or the Black Watch on the collar, but they all wear the same Glengarry. This means that the Argyll and Sutherland Highlanders' Glengarry has gone along with their badge. Everyone is now wearing a single new cap badge.' Indeed, when the former British Secretary of State for Defence, Geoff Hoon, announced the formation of the Royal Regiment of Scotland in December 2004 it caused a furore among many soldiers, veterans and the public alike, north and south of the border. One reason for this was that one of the regiments faced with amalgamation into the new 'super regiment', the Black Watch, was then on duty in Iraq. At the time some said that the soldiers of this fine regiment had been 'stabbed in the back'. Another concern was that the new regiment is to wear the kilt, the traditional garb of Highland soldiers, on ceremonial occasions. However, some of its component units are Lowland troops (such as the Royal Scots) who traditionally wear the tartan trews. Many think that the whole ethos of Lowland units could be subsumed into a Highland ethos.

The brand new cap badge was revealed in August 2005. Its design incorporates the saltire of St Andrew upon which the lion rampant is shown. Because it is a Royal regiment, the badge is surmounted by a crown, but the crown of Scotland. The new unit consists of a total of five battalions, four from one each of the then remaining Scottish regiments and one from the combination of the Royal Scots and the King's Own Scottish Borderers. The Royal Regiment of Scotland is now the senior line infantry regiment (and the only Scottish regiment) in the British Army. Its motto, *Nemo Me Impune Lacessit* ('No one assaults me with impunity') is the same wording as that previously used by the Royal Scots, the Royal Highland Fusiliers and the Black Watch.

It is ironic that it is only the brand-new badges that are highly sought and, because of the new strict regulations preventing official emblems of British security forces falling into the wrong hands (a product of 'The War on Terror'), in limited supply. Because so many of the cap badges of the six regiments comprising the Royal Regiment of Scotland, for example, will now naturally find their way into the trade, these badges, which until recently commanded relatively high prices, will now be quite common.

While I was visiting Sabre Sales to talk to Nick Hall, I had the good fortune to meet Chris Toft, a friend of his and a fellow badge collector specializing in cloth badges. Although most British cap badges were, of course, manufactured from metal, some, most notably those worn by officers or those in Special Forces and then post-Second World War, were manufactured from cloth.

Toft told me that he started collecting badges in 1976, when he was serving in the Military Police. 'I was the local policeman for Hounslow and initially no one spoke to me when I was going around the local military clothing stores on duty, but I found that, when I started collecting badges, people thought, "He can't be as bad as all that" and they started speaking to me.'

Mint and unissued post-Second World War khaki drill sergeant major's crown.

Cloth badge enthusiast Chris Toft.

Toft then joined his local militaria society in London, at first collecting cap badges until he became disillusioned upon discovering that, because somebody had bought all the original dies (*see* my earlier discussion with Hall), 'old' badges were still being manufactured unofficially. Then, finding that a great many of the badges he had swapped other items for, were effectively reproduction – and not liking repro badges – Toft, who already had a large collection of cloth badges, decided to concentrate solely on fabric items.

'Today, quite a lot of the other ranks' beret badges are manufactured from woven cloth, mainly because they don't break when they are being worn', Toft said, 'However, originally it was officers and senior NCOs who had embroidered beret badges. Today, officers wear berets and what they call the "chip bag" hat, which is a slouch hat on which they wear gold-wire embroidered badges. I suppose the hardest to find and the most rare twentieth-century cloth badges would include the yeomanry, TA and volunteer regiments, although I have only ever seen one genuine Second World War cloth SAS badge, so these are obviously quite rare too. Wartime general officers' embroidered badges are hard to find too.'

I asked Toft how much of a problem moths were to cloth badges. 'Moths are attracted to certain kinds of cloth, not the embroidered wire, but certainly the fabric backing that holds the badge together. But, if you mount your badges on A4 or A3 sheets (I use Sellotape doubled over to lightly hold them in place), store them in transparent, plastic pockets and put them away

ABOVE: **Signals qualification emblems worn above rank insignia (chevrons) to denote attendance at, in this case, the Hythe Signals Wing.**

BELOW: **Women's Land Army auxiliary general service emblem as worn on the unit's pullovers.**

ABOVE: Second World War Women's Voluntary Service (WVS) rank brassard. Such Civil Defence (CD) and National Service items are now much coveted by collectors.

BELOW: Mint and un-issued post-Second World War line infantry WOI Regimental Sergeant Major (RSM) sleeve emblem.

somewhere dry you shouldn't have any problems', he said.

'However, if you use Blu-Tack or double-sided sticky tape to hold the badges in place, I find that it can ruin their backs. If it is an especially thin badge, like many I have collected in the past, these alternative adhesives, especially Blu-Tack which is an oily substance, tend to leave traces on the badge, which can't be removed. The only problem with my method of holding things in place with Sellotape is that it does tear any paper backing from the badges should you try to remove them from the display sheets. But if left in place – no problem.'

Toft told me that his method of storage and display was not only space efficient and neat, it made exhibiting or discussing his collection with like-minded enthusiasts really easy. 'You just sling your book out. There it is and they turn it over a page at a time seeing what you have got.'

Like all collectors, Toft has a permanent collection he intends to keep and add to and he supports his hobby by selling or swapping from a reserve of badges he has accumulated over the years. His pride and joy numbers about 1,000 cloth badges, but he can call on a reserve of ten times this number to help to support his hobby.

I asked Toft whether he was looking for any particular badges that were not currently in his collection. He told me that, like most collectors, his goals, ambitions and specific interests changed from time to time and that there was always something that he was after. 'At the moment I am collecting the modern TRF [Tactical Recognition Flashes] that the regular Army wears today. There are still quite a few of these that I would like in my collection. Unfortunately, finding the real stuff these days is getting harder and harder.'

He purchases many of his badges from the militaria fairs he attends regularly up and down the country. 'You just look around. I know a lot of the dealers and some of them save me things. People might come up offering to sell or exchange badges. Unfortunately, shops like Nick's [Sabre Sales] are increasingly few and far between.' Toft told me that in the future he hopes to produce a book about reproduction insignia, something he feels most strongly about. 'It's wrong because they are fleecing the customer. I know a lot of dealers who point out when something is repro and not original, but there a lot who aren't quite as honest about that distinction.'

BADGE COLLECTING: THE EVOLUTION OF THE BRITISH ARMY CAP BADGE IN THE TWENTIETH CENTURY

This chapter considers the principal changes in the design of cap badges in the twentieth century. Principally this means the move from large badges worn on 'blue cloth' helmets at the beginning of the period – a remnant of Napoleonic shako plates – to smaller, lighter and cheaper anodized aluminium, or higher quality but privately purchased, gilding metal cap badges, universally worn during the last quarter of the century.

During this period alone, if the collector opted for only one or two regiments, there would be a wide choice of styles and finishes from which to choose and build a themed collection. Indeed, to illustrate more clearly the changes in cap badge design throughout the twentieth century, I have selected one regiment, the Royal Hampshire Regiment (which amalgamated with The Queens in 1992 to form The Princess of Wales's Royal Regiment), and what is now a corps, the Royal Artillery, to show the principal developments. (*See* pages 56–61 and 63–6.)

The regimental structure of the Army is dynamic. New regiments are continually being formed, usually because of amalgamations. In fact, one could argue that the Army is in a more volatile state today than ever before. There are two aspects to this: first, the twenty-first-century creation of super regiments has created many new badges and consigned many to the archives (a benefit to collectors of limited edition items) and, secondly, the dramatic changes that have

forced previously proudly independent regiments – especially those in Scotland – to join forces with others with the natural loss of at least some distinctiveness has created havoc in the ranks and especially with veterans' groups.

Anodized badge of the Highland Brigade (with hackle) worn between 1959 and 1968.

The Home Counties Brigade formally came into being on 14 October 1959. The badge features a sword piercing a Saxon crown, symbolizing the ancient linkages between Middlesex, Kent, Surrey and Sussex. Soldiers from these county regiments wore this badge (it was not popular) alongside their individual shoulder titles and, uniquely on battledress, their own collar badges. The formation of The Queen's Regiment in 1966 made this badge obsolete.

Anodized version of the Royal Scots badge offset by scarlet backing behind.

Bimetal cap badge of The Royal Scots (The Royal Regiment), the oldest infantry regiment of the line in the Army (raised in 1633 by Sir John Hepburn). While serving in Sweden and France in the seventeenth century it was known as the Dumbarton Regiment, but gained the name The Royal Regiment following its service at Tangier in 1680. In 1983 the regiment celebrated its 350th anniversary when the Queen named the Princess Royal to be Colonel in Chief. The Royal Scots battalion is now part of The Royal Regiment of Scotland.

All ranks' bronze metal cap badge of the Princess of
Wales's Royal Regiment. This is worn on the beret,
backed by a square of alternating blue and yellow silk.

ABOVE: **Princess of Wales's Royal Regiment soldier's
bright metal cap badge.**

BELOW: **Queen's Regiment bimetal cap badge from the
1970s.**

Although this work focuses on twentieth-century
badges, to put things in their proper context it is
important to mention the handful of new super regiments that characterize the redevelopment of the
British Army in the twenty-first century and are the
result of implementation of the government's Future
Army Structure (FAS), a programme intended to
develop a more deployable, flexible and, above all,
agile army. It is arguable of course, that such regiments
are not new and one could cite the creation of the
Royal Anglian Regiment in 1964 as the first major step
towards the creation of such larger units, followed by
the formation of The Queen's Regiment in 1966 from
the old Home Counties Brigade and then the creation
of The Princess of Wales's Royal Regiment, a union of
The Queens and the Royal Hampshire Regiment in
1992. Understanding such evolution helps the reader
to appreciate the context of the new regimental structure and to find out where within it a particular unit
and its badge might fit.

Enter the Badge

Although the term 'badge' in reference to regimental emblems first appears in a Royal Warrant dating from 1751, it was not until nearly fifty years later with the introduction of the shako that cap badges came into general use in the British Army. Effectively, shako plates were the precursors of modern cap badges. Before this the Army's soft, broad-brimmed, two- and three-pointed hats (bicorns and tricorns) had proved unsuitable for the application of regalia. However, some headdress insignia were employed before the widespread introduction of the shako. Initially worn by Grenadiers – who found the ubiquitous, wide-brimmed hats an encumbrance when throwing their grenades – a tall fur cap was employed to mitigate this problem. Interestingly, the wide-brimmed hats also made it difficult for soldiers to sling their arms without

knocking off their headdress and consequently other regiments began to adopt this form of headgear, the stiffened front flaps of these fur caps proving ideal for the display of the royal cipher or crown.

Naturally enough, flaming grenades, the emblems of their trade, were adopted alongside other badges, including the royal arms and national insignia such as shamrocks. Likewise, fusiliers and light dragoons adopted distinctive helmet adornments (the dragoons, particularly, also adopted distinctive helmets combining fur crests and turbans). Indeed, the 1751 Warrant included the Duke of Cumberland's suggestion that a number indicating a unit's precedence should be more prominently displayed on regimental colours and quickly these numbers became prominent elements of headdress insignia when used.

However, while most soldiers wore soft, wide-brimmed headdress, what badges there were in the

LEFT: **Cap badge of the Royal Scots Fusiliers with a King's crown. They achieved Royal status in 1712. One of their nicknames is Marlborough's Own. In 1959 they amalgamated with the Highland Light Infantry becoming the Royal Highland Fusiliers.**

BELOW: **A very old badge with a Queen's (Victoria's) crown. It belongs to The Wiltshire Regiment.**

modern sense were more often than not attached to a soldier's leather cartridge pouch or a cavalry officer's sabretache.

The Shako

All this changed at the beginning of the nineteenth century, on 24 February 1800 when an Army Order decreed that British infantry regiments would adopt the shako. This tall, cylindrical helmet was copied from the headdress long worn by Hungarian Magyars and which had also been adopted by Austrian troops. Nicknamed the 'stovepipe' by British troops, this helmet lent itself admirably to adornment. Regimental helmet plates and plumes – red and white for most troops, dark green for light companies and white for grenadiers – completed the transformation.

Helmet plates were quite different from modern badges, however. Indeed, they were 6in tall and some 4in wide – the shako itself being 8in tall. Though still much larger than twentieth-century cap badges, the insignia worn on the shorter Albert shakos of the 1850s and the cap-like militia shakos that followed

(many influenced by the French kepi) began to more closely resemble modern badges, generally consisting of an eight-pointed star surmounted by the monarch's crown. The shako persisted in one form or another until the 1870s, when it was replaced by a more rounded helmet based on the headdress worn by Prussian troops and the spike-topped helmets adopted by Metropolitan Police in the 1860s. In 1878 an Army Order made the wearing of these helmets mandatory throughout the British Army. Constructed of cork and covered with blue cloth for most units but green for light infantry, this helmet was generally surmounted by a teutonic spike. Specialist corps such as the artillery and the engineers wore helmets surmounted by a distinctive ball in a leaf cup.

Redesigning the Army

The style and composition of helmets and the design of the insignia worn on them were not the only things that were changing significantly in the British Army at this time. In 1868 the Secretary of State Edward Cardwell began to create a modern army, abolishing flogging for

An old and rare badge belonging to the Lancashire Hussars Imperial Yeomanry.

Queen Victoria's crown (QVC) surmounts the badge of the Royal Gloucestershire Hussars, a yeomanry regiment.

In response to explosions on the British mainland in the 1860s, the Post Office Rifles were formed when 1,600 Post Office staff were enrolled as Special Constables. After several alterations to its name, a permanent regiment was formed, becoming in 1880 the 24th Middlesex Rifle Volunteers (Post Office Rifles). Following the Reserve Forces Bill of 1907, in 1908 this unit became the 8th Battalion, City of London Regiment (Post Office Rifles). The very rare badge shown here features a Queen's crown (QVC).

miscreants and the much abused practice whereby the wealthy could purchase commissions. He also set about reinforcing the territorial links between a regiment and the neighbouring area from where its recruits came.

In 1881 Hugh Childers, then Secretary of State, picked up where Cardwell left off and made even more dramatic recommendations. His General Order of May 1881 finally put paid to the importance of regimental numbers as far as insignia were concerned. Instead, he decreed that regiments would be known by their regimental titles. In order to manage this change efficiently within counties with several numbered regiments, amalgamations would be required. Although they caused much disquiet, these reforms went ahead and paved the way for the regimental system with which the British Army entered the twentieth century.

Three further dramatic changes to headdress were introduced at the end of the nineteenth century, each greatly influencing the design of cap badges during the subsequent century. The first of these was the Glengarry, a Scottish-style bonnet adopted in 1868 for undress wear by all British regiments (although English regiments ceased to wear it in the 1890s). The second major development was the introduction of the present style of peaked cap in 1898. With its wide circular

Brass cap badge of the Royal Berkshire (Hungerford) Yeomanry (Dragoons). This was in use between 1908 and 1922 but not to be confused with the even more rare and similar Berkshire Imperial Yeomanry badge it replaced.

ABOVE: **Brass cap badge of The Queen's Royal Regiment (West Surrey), adopted in 1924. The regiment amalgamated with the East Surreys in 1959.**

BELOW: **In 1881 the successors of the Old Tangier Regiment of Foot (raised in 1661) and Villiers' Regiment of Marines became the 1st and 2nd Battalions of the East Surrey Regiment. Their battle honours testify to their mottos: Pristinae Virtutis Memor ('Mindful of the gallant actions of the past') and Vel Exuvia Triumphans ('Even in defeat there can be triumph').**

top, this design influenced the service cap of the First World War and beyond and the current No.2 dress cap worn by modern troops on ceremonial occasions. At first, officers and NCOs wore the peaked version of this cap only, other ranks making do with a peakless version, the Broderick. This was unpopular, however, and was retained only by the Royal Marine Light Infantry. The final universal development was the introduction of the flat, folding Field Service Cap, a development of the old forage caps worn by troops when on manoeuvres or active service. In 1937 a coloured version of this was introduced, the colour of the crown indicating the particular regiment. These caps endured throughout two world wars, although the introduction of berets – black for the Tank Corps in 1924 and red and green for the Parachute Regiment and the Commandos, respectively, in the 1940s heralded their end.

Precedence

The most logical way to study the changes in the design and variety of cap badges in the twentieth century is to consider the badges of the principal regiments as the cavalry and infantry regiments are listed in order of precedence. This order relates to the date, often hundreds of years ago, when individual regiments were first

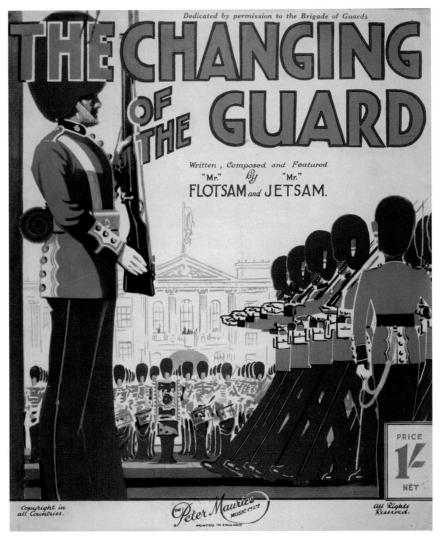

The Brigade of Guards have always had an appeal, especially to visitors from overseas, somewhat lacking in other formations, as this 1940s song sheet testifies.

raised. It even supersedes Cardwell's 1881 abolition of the system of numbering regiments and is why The Princess of Wales's Royal Regiment (PWRR), one of the newest in the Army, is ranked second in the order of precedence of infantry regiments. Although the PWRR was formed as recently as 1992, it came from the amalgamation of The Queen's Regiment and the Royal Hampshire Regiment, elements of which could trace themselves back to the formation of The Queen's Royal Regiment of Foot (classified the 2nd of Foot when regimental numbering was introduced in Britain in 1751).

For simplicity, I have decided to look at the principal cap badges of the corps within the British Army, considering in detail some of the badges of the famous cavalry and infantry regiments that have now been absorbed into, for example, components of the Royal Armoured Corps, the Foot Guards and the regiments of line infantry.

Many of the developmental changes in badge design, from the reduction in size of those worn on the early 'blue cloth' helmets at the start of the period covered here, through developments in brass, bimetal, cloth, embroidered wire and anodized aluminium badges that occurred simultaneously throughout the Army. Therefore, even if the specific design of individual badges varied, many of the changes took place en masse, affecting the insignia of most regiments at the same time. Individual peculiarities and differences are best discovered by studying the accompanying photographs and captions.

The Cavalry and the Armoured Forces

So, following the usual order of precedence, we begin by looking at the badge of the most senior unit in the British Army, those of the Household Cavalry. Combined, the Life Guards and The Blues and Royals (Royal Horse Guards and 1st The Royal Dragoons) constitute the Household Cavalry. They are the oldest and most senior regiments in the Army and can trace their heritage back to 1660. In its operational role today, the Household Cavalry Regiment serves in armoured fighting vehicles, and earned distinction in the Falklands in 1982, the Gulf in 1990 and later in Bosnia and Kosovo. Five Foot Guard regiments form the Household Division. The Household Cavalry Mounted Regiment is equipped with horses and carries out ceremonial duties on state occasions, such as providing the Sovereign's Escort at the annual Queen's Birthday Parade in June.

Famous for their scarlet-plumed (Blues and Royals) or white-plumed (Lifeguards) helmets, bearing similar insignia which change only upon the accession of a new monarch, it was not until 1913 that a cap badge proper was introduced and this was only because, when not on ceremonial duty, units of the Household Cavalry wore khaki for the first time.

Two types of badge were produced. One, for wear on the service dress cap, featuring the monarch's cipher surrounded by a circlet bearing the title of the regiment and the imperial crown, was ready in time for the outbreak of the Great War in 1914; the other, worn on the forage cap, which was reissued in 1919, featured the royal cipher surrounded by the garter.

The Royal Horse Artillery is next in order of precedence. Today, the 1st and 3rd Regiments Royal Horse

A white metal King's crown Second World War beret badge of the Royal Armoured Corps (RAC).

Artillery (1 RHA and 3 RHA) comprise the senior units within the Royal Regiment of Artillery (RA). There are two other RHA regiments within the RA and each wears the distinctive badge featuring the oval monarch's cipher and garter surmounted by a Queen's crown. When worn in conjunction with the RA's distinctive cannon cap badge, on the No.2 dress cap, for example, members of the RHA wear their unit's own badge on collar lapels.

Although it did not exist until 4 April 1939, with its mailed fist cap badge the Royal Armoured Corps (RAC) is next in precedence in parade order within the Army. The corps has been constituted from the old cavalry regiments, including the famous Royal Scots Dragoon Guards (Carabiniers and Greys) and the 9th/12th Royal Lancers (Prince of Wales's) and some equally renowned yeomanry regiments such as the Royal Wessex Yeomanry and the Royal Mercian and Lancastrian Yeomanry. Today, the RAC provides the muscle of the British Army with its constituent regiments being

ABOVE: **Cap badge of the 11th (Prince Albert's Own) Hussars, worn until 1969.**

LEFT: **King's crown cap badge of The King's Dragoon Guards.**

Featuring a relief of Enniskillen Castle, this is the cap badge of the 6th (Inniskilling) Dragoons. The keep of this castle houses the museum of another famous regiment from the region – The Royal Inniskilling Fusiliers.

either armoured and operating main battle tanks (MBTs) such as the Challenger II or formation reconnaissance and equipped with Scimitar armoured fighting vehicles (AFVs).

The individual badges of the cavalry regiments within the RAC are immediately distinctive and striking, the badge of The Queen's Dragoon Guards, for example, still features the Imperial Eagle from the badge of the 1st King's Dragoon Guards (KDG). This eagle was taken from the arms of Emperor Francis Joseph 1 of Austria who was Colonel-in-Chief of the regiment in 1896, the year 'modern' cap badges were fully introduced. Because of anti-German sentiment between 1915 and 1937, this motif was dropped in favour of a simple star design, but it returned until the KDG and the Queen's Bays (2nd Dragoon Guards, whose badge featured the word *Bays* in old English script within a laurel wreath and surmounted by a crown) amalgamated to form The Queen's Dragoon Guards in 1959.

Featuring the Napoleonic eagle captured by Sgt Ewart at the Battle of Waterloo, the badge of the Royal Scots Dragoon Guards harks back to the days of the Royal Scots Greys. The crossed carbines beneath the eagle are from the badge of the 3rd Carabiniers (Prince of Wales's Dragoon Guards), the Greys and the Carabineers having amalgamated in 1971 to form the Royal Scots Dragoon Guards.

In 1992 the 4th/7th Royal Dragoon Guards and the 5th Royal Inniskillling Dragoon Guards amalgamated to form the Royal Dragoon Guards. Their cap badge combines the star of the Order of St Patrick from the badge of the 4th/7th with a depiction of Enniskilling Castle from that of the 5th.

The following year The Queen's Own Hussars and The Queen's Royal Irish Lancers amalgamated to form The Queen's Royal Hussars (The Queen's Own and Royal Irish). Their cap badge combines the Irish harp from the original King's Royal Irish Hussars badge backed by the monogram of the 7th Queen's Own Hussars.

The badge of the next cavalry regiment according to precedence in the RAC, the 9th/12th Royal Lancers (Prince of Wales's), was adopted in 1960 when the 9th Queen's Royal lancers and the 12th Royal Lancers were amalgamated. Before then the badge of the 9th featured crossed lances with a central number '9' and the 12th, the Prince of Wales's feathers backed by crossed lances and surmounted by a crown. The current badge is based on that of the old 12th Lancers badge, but with the number 'IX/XII' in a scroll at the badge base.

Known in the regiment as 'The Hawk', the badge of The King's Royal Hussars features the Prussian eagle of Princess Frederica Charlotte; she married the Duke of York in 1798, when the forebears of the regiment were called The Duchess of York's Own. Although it was discontinued during and immediately after the First World War because of anti-German feeling, this eagle is still the principal element of The King's Royal Hussars' badge, despite its originally being the emblem of the

The Prince of Wales's feathers above the cap badge of the 12th Royal Lancers.

Rare cap badge of the 14th (King's) Hussars, disbanded in 1915 and consequently quite rare.

14th/20th Hussars, who amalgamated with The Royal Hussars in 1992 to form the new regiment. However, the Prince of Wales's plumes of the old Royal Hussars' badge are worn as regimental collar emblems.

Based on the Maltese cross design featured on shako plates before the light dragoon regiments converted to hussars in the nineteenth century, the badge of the Light Dragoons, formed by the amalgamation of the 13th/18th Royal Hussars and the 15th/19th The King's Royal Hussars, was introduced in 1992.

Perhaps one of the most striking cavalry cap badges in the Army is that of the Queen's Royal Lancers. Featuring a striking death's head, crossbones and the motto *Or Glory*, this badge is based on the device of the 17th Lancers and dates from the eighteenth century. The skull and crossbones device was retained on the 17th's merger with the 21st in 1922 and again in 1993 when The Queen's Royal Lancers was formed. The badge of the 16th/5th The Queen's Royal Lancers (featuring the linked garter and cipher of Queen Charlotte, from the original badge of the 16th with the Order of St Patrick from the old 5th Royal Irish lancers) is worn as the new regiment's collar badge.

In 1922 the 17th (Duke of Cambridge's Own Lancers) and the 21st Empress of India's Lancers amalgamated to form the 17th/21st Lancers. This is a Second World War vintage white metal cap badge.

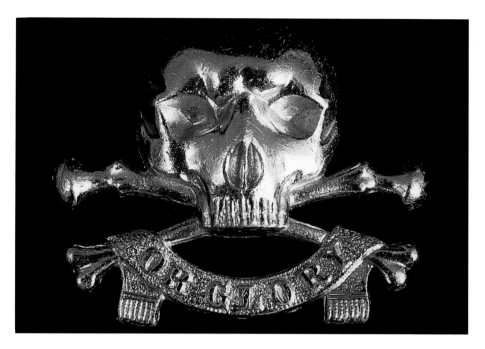

1960s anodized aluminium Staybrite cap badge of the 17th/21st Lancers.

The RAC incorporates the Royal Tank Regiment (formerly the Tank Corps and then the Royal Tank Corps), the possessors of the famous cap badge featuring an outline of one of the rhomboid-shaped tanks Britain introduced during the Great War.

This cap badge is directly related to another famous one illustrated here – that of the Machine Gun Corps (MGC). The Corps was established in 1915, with three components: Cavalry, Infantry and Motor Machine Gun Services. The brass crossed Vickers machine guns

ABOVE: **King's crown white metal beret badge of the Royal Tank Regiment, which became an independent regiment after the Great War in which it was known as the Royal Tank Corps. Featuring a depiction of one of the rhomboid vehicles used in the First World War, the regiment's motto is appropriate: 'Fear Naught'.**

RIGHT: **Brass cap badge showing the twin Vickers machine-guns of the Machine Gun Corps. This unit existed between 1915 and 1922 and consequently the badge has become increasingly hard to find.**

ABOVE: Bimetal cap badge of the 3rd King's Own Hussars. Though the regiment was formed at the start of the standing army in 1685, British hussars were not introduced until 1806, the regiment taking the name above in 1861. The badge features the white horse of Hanover. The 3rd King's Own became an armoured car unit in 1936 but had tanks by the time of the battle of El Alamein in 1942.

LEFT: Very rare Guards Machine Gun Regiment cap badge. This unit was raised in 1916 and disbanded in 1920.

surmounted by the crown, cap badge of the MGC, is a sought-after collectable; the Corps was disbanded in 1922.

It was the Heavy Branch of the MGC that operated six tank companies at the battle of Flers in 1916, but it was not until July 1917 that the Branch was officially separated from the MGC, renamed the Tank Corps and awarded its distinctive badge. The Tank Corps become the Royal Tank Corps in 1923 and the Royal Tank Regiment in 1939, as it is today, keeping its distinctive badge throughout.

Artillery and Engineers

As strikingly memorable as the Royal Tank Regiment's badge, that of the next corps in order of precedence, the Royal Artillery (RA, motto Quo Fas Et Gloria

Ducunt, 'Where Duty and Glory Lead'), is equally recognizable. Worn since 1903, when service dress was first introduced, this badge features a muzzle-loading, 9-pounder field piece dating from 1871. This gun equipped Queen Victoria's Horse and Field artillery.

Brass King's crown Royal Artillery cap badge.

Anodized Queen's crown Royal Artillery cap badge.

THE BADGES OF THE ARTILLERY

The ubiquitous blue cloth helmet was the standard headdress of British soldiers at the turn of the twentieth century. This rare Victorian helmet plate belongs to a volunteer artillery officer.

Pre-1922 Royal Marine Artillery other ranks' blue cloth helmet badge.

Victorian regular artillery officer's pouch badge.

The images in this section are intended to show the step-by-step development of the badges throughout the twentieth century, from that worn on the blue cloth helmets at the turn of the century through to the more famous gun badges of the Corps of the Royal Artillery. Also shown are specific rarities from the Honourable Artillery Company (HAC), the Royal Horse Artillery, the Royal Marine Artillery and the Royal Garrison Artillery, as well as the badge unique to Canadian gunners in the First World War.

Until the early eighteenth century artillery 'traynes' were raised by Royal Warrant on an ad hoc basis as campaigning required. Following the establishment of two regular companies of field artillery at Woolwich and their grouping with independent artillery units on Gibraltar and Minorca, in 1722, the Royal Regiment of Artillery was established. In 1793 four troops of Royal Horse Artillery were formed in support of the cavalry. On 1 July 1899 the Royal Artillery was divided into two

Second World War Royal Horse Artillery service cap badge (George VI crown).

HAC Infantry Section badge. The grenade badge was taken from their sponsors, the Grenadier Guards.

First of three King's crown variations of the Honourable Artillery Company's cap badge – the gun badge.

continued overleaf

THE BADGES OF THE ARTILLERY *continued*

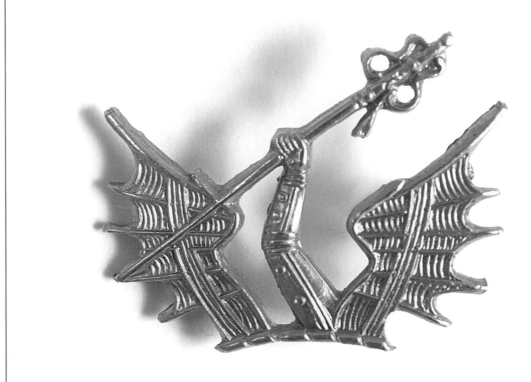

LEFT: Standard cap badge as worn from 1924 when the Royal Field Artillery and the Royal Garrison Artillery were united into a single corps – the Royal Artillery; the Latin motto Quo Fas Et Gloria Ducunt means 'Whither Right and Glory Lead'.

BELOW: HAC beret badge.

Beginning life as a collar badge, the classic Royal Artillery grenade emblem effectively became the Corps' cap badge throughout the Second World War when worn on the unit's field service cap.

This Bakelite version of the badge on the left was a Second World War economy measure. A similar plastic version of the Royal Artillery's iconic gun badge was also produced but is now extremely rare.

Effectively a small-scale version of the standard cap badge, this King's crown small gun badge was the unit's first beret badge. It became the Queen's crown and was anodized in the 1950s.

continued overleaf

THE BADGES OF THE ARTILLERY *continued*

Modern, full-sized, anodized Royal Artillery other ranks' cap badge.

Unusual artillery militia badge dating from 1901–08 and featuring an Edwardian crown. The more common versions of this badge carry laurels as opposed to *Ubique* ('Everywhere') in the scroll above the design.

Royal Artillery cap badge belonging to a Maltese battery.

1st Battalion Hampshire Royal Garrison Artillery Volunteer's cap badge. Collectors should note the variety of scroll variations denoting different units.

Standard white metal Volunteers badge dating from the First World War, in other words, post-1908 and the Haldane reforms, as opposed to the pre-1908 militia.

groups: the Royal Horse Artillery and the Royal Field Artillery comprised one group, while the coastal defence, mountain, siege and heavy batteries formed another group named the Royal Garrison Artillery. The three sections effectively functioned as separate corps. In common with much of the rest of the Army, the artillery depended on volunteers to help to fill its ranks. However, this civilian-administered system was subject

The Canadian Commonwealth badge was unique to the First World War; in the Second World War Canadian gunners wore an identical badge to British artillerymen.

The Ayrshire (Earl of Carrick's Own) Yeomanry is Scotland's senior yeomanry unit with an unbroken history dating back to 1793. During the First World War they served at Gallipoli and in Egypt as a yeomanry battalion of the Royal Scots Fusiliers and during the Second World War as a yeomanry field regiment in the Royal Artillery. In 1949 they were reformed as a unit of the Royal Armoured Corps. This anodized cap badge dates from the late 1950s.

to abuse and potential financial insolvency and in 1908 the government took over the volunteer army completely, reorganizing it as the Territorial Force. Consequently many volunteer artillery units such as the 1st Hampshire Royal Garrison Artillery (V) changed titles.

The 1899 reorganization endured until 1924, when the RFA and the RGA were united with the Royal Artillery proper. However, the Royal Horse Artillery, which has always had its own separate traditions, uniforms and insignia, retained a separate elite identity, which remains to this day. Although operationally part of the RA's order of battle, today four separate Royal Horse Artillery regiments wear the cipher cap badge, among them the most famous is The King' Troop. When on parade with its guns, the Royal Horse Artillery takes precedence over every other regiment and corps in the Army and parades at the right of the line, otherwise, it immediately follows the Household Cavalry.

Royal Artillery officer's coloured field service cap with wire badge.

At various times during the twentieth century this gun was depicted in differing depths of relief and on occasions the gun's wheel was free to rotate. The first Queen's crown (St Edward's crown) badge was made available in 1955; the current anodized version was introduced in 1958. Today officers wear a wire-embroidered beret badge and soldiers have the opportunity to purchase privately gilding metal beret badges that are superior in quality to the anodized versions.

The cap badge of the Corps of Royal Engineers (RE), or Sappers as they are more commonly known, features a royal cipher surmounted by a crown, both of which change with the accession of a new monarch, all surrounded by the garter and laurel leaves. The current design was adopted in 1898, though the design is similar to that on the badge worn by the Royal Sappers and Miners in the 1820s.

As an economy measure during the First World War the central area around the cipher was 'unvoided' (solid) and at others it was pierced ('voided'). In the Second World War a different economy measure was introduced. Then, as with so many other famous badges, the Royal Engineers' badges were produced from plastics, saving precious brass for the manufacture of shell and cartridge cases.

Formed in 1920 from the Royal Engineers Signal Service, the Royal Corps of Signals is responsible for installing, maintaining and operating the Army's telecommunications infrastructure. Its cap badge features Mercury, messenger of the gods, carrying the caduceus (the classical herald's wand). The Corps' motto is *Certa Cito*, 'Swift and Sure'.

The Infantry

Currently there are fifty battalions of infantry formed from the eighteen regiments in the Army. Thirty-six of these are regular and fourteen are part-time territorial units.

First in order of precedence in the infantry are the Foot Guards of the Household Division. There are five regiments of Foot Guards (a sixth, the Guards Machine Gun Regiment was formed during the First World War and disbanded in 1920) and their badges have remained unchanged during the twentieth century. Indeed, the badge of the Grenadier Guards, a flaming grenade, has changed little since it was introduced following the Battle of Waterloo, when it replaced the

The King's cipher and wreath of a Second World War cap badge of the Corps of Royal Engineers. Engineers have served in every theatre since their formation in 1683.

THE BADGES OF THE ROYAL HAMPSHIRE REGIMENT

Victorian Royal Hampshire Regiment officer's blue cloth helmet plate (1881–1901).

Edwardian Hampshire other ranks' blue cloth helmet plate (1902–14).

Other ranks' Royal Hampshire Regiment glengarry badge 1880s–90s.

This selection, like those of the Artillery, is intended to illustrate the steady progression of cap badge design from the elaborate plates worn on blue cloth helmets at the end of the nineteenth century and the turn of the twentieth through those worn by the Hampshire Regiment through two world wars until their incorporation, with The Queen's Regiment, into the new Princess of Wales's Royal Regiment in the early 1990s.

Raised in Ireland in 1702 during the war of the Spanish Succession (1701–19) and known as Meredith's Regiment, in 1751 it became the 37th Foot, which in 1782, became the North Hampshire Regiment with the South Hampshire Regiment being classified the 67th Foot. After twenty-one years in India under active service conditions, the 67th returned to England in 1826, and, in commemoration of this, George IV authorized the figure of the Royal tiger with the word India superscribed to be borne on its colours and appointments, hence the

continued overleaf

THE BADGES OF THE ROYAL HAMPSHIRE REGIMENT *continued*

ABOVE: **All-brass economy Royal Hampshire Regiment other ranks' cap badge from 1916.**

LEFT: **Officer's silver-gilt and enamel Royal Hampshire Regiment forage cap (peaked headdress) and glengarry badge from the 1880s–90s.**

Other ranks' 1890s blue field service Royal Hampshire Regiment cap badge; this is a specific badge as opposed to a collar badge, as the uninitiated might suppose.

Second World War economy Royal Hampshire Regiment Bakelite cap badge; all such cheaply produced war economy badges are now rare and expensive.

Royal Hampshire Regiment officer's silver-gilt and enamel peaked cap badge (post-First World War No.1 dress badge).

nickname the 'Tigers', still used today. In 1881 the 37th North Hampshire and the 67th South Hampshire Regiment were united under the title of the 1st and 2nd Battalion, the Hampshire Regiment. The different cap badges worn by officers and soldiers date from this time.

In 1949 the Hampshire Regiment was reduced to only one battalion and then in 1970 to only one company, the Minden Company (in honour of the 37th's valiant action at the battle of Minden in 1759; the Regiment wears a 'Minden' rose in its headdress on 1 August each year, in memory of the men who picked roses as they returned from the battle).

In 1970 the regiment returned to battalion strength and in 1985, while stationed in Berlin, the Princess of Wales was appointed its Colonel in Chief. The regiment amalgamated with The Queen's Regiment in 1992 to form a new regiment of two battalions entitled The Princess of Wales's Royal Regiment

Royal Hampshire Regiment officer's silver-gilt and enamel No.1 dress King's crown cap badge (1947–53).

continued overleaf

THE BADGES OF THE ROYAL HAMPSHIRE REGIMENT *continued*

ABOVE: **Royal Hampshire Regiment officer's wire beret badge worn from the 1960s to the 1990s.**

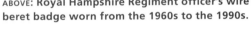

LEFT: **Very rare – the badge of the 'amalgamation that never happened' – the proposed combination of the Hampshires with the Gloucestershire Regiment, the decision to unite these was reversed in 1970 and consequently, this badge is highly prized by collectors.**

BELOW LEFT: **A selection of Royal Hampshire Regiment Territorial cap badges (1908–60s). Clockwise from top left: cap badge worn by the 6th Battalion (Duke of Connaught's) 1908–37, Second World War period 6th Battalion cap badge, 7th Battalion cap badge, 8th Battalion cap badge, 9th Battalion cap badge, officers' pattern 6th Battalion cap badge.**

(Queen's and Royal Hampshires). The Hampshire's military service is one of the most glorious in the Army, including actions at Blenheim (1704), Ramillies (1706), Oudenarde (1708) and Malplaquet (1709). Recalling an earlier event, the Hampshire rose in the Regiment's cap badge design commemorates the rose awarded to the trained bands of Hampshire who fought for Henry V at Agincourt in 1415.

The 2nd Battalion served in the South African War from 1900 to 1902 – the bronze badges and buttons worn by officers dating from this campaign. During the Great War the Regiment fielded thirty-six battalions, the 2nd winning honours at Gallipoli. During the next war the Regiment served with distinction in North Africa, Sicily, Italy, Greece and on D-Day; in 1946 George VI was 'graciously pleased to approve that the Regiment shall enjoy the distinction of Royal'. In the 1960s and the 1970s the Regiment served in Northern Ireland. The Regiment has gained ten Victoria Crosses during its history, four at the capture of the Taku Forts in 1860, three in the Great War and three in the Second World War.

Bringing the story up to date: the cap badge of The Rifles, the largest infantry super regiment in the Army and formed on 1 February 2007 from the following regiments: the Devonshire and Dorset Light Infantry, the Royal Gloucestershire, Berkshire and Wiltshire Light Infantry, the Light Infantry and the Royal Green Jackets. In consequence the new regiment will share 437 battle honours and 118 Victoria Crosses. Each soldier in the Rifles has the right to call himself Rifleman, an honour previously only accorded to the Royal Green Jackets.

royal cipher and crown. The current design of the Grenadier Guards badge dates from 1952, being produced for George VI's funeral. Interestingly the Grenadiers' badge escaped ever being made from anodized aluminium, the bowl of the grenade's orb being too deep to mould in this lighter alloy and the regiment's cap badge is still made from gilding metal. Officers wear wire-embroidered interpretations of the cap badge on all caps and berets. Uniquely, the ranks of Guardsmen are also displayed by an arrangement of bands on the peaks of their forage caps (as well as with chevrons and on epaulettes and collars, of course).

The distinctive star of the Order of the Garter badge worn by the Coldstream Guards was granted to the regiment by William III in 1696, making it the oldest regimental badge in the Army. A variety of versions of this famous badge are worn including anodized, silver and enamel (battalion staff), officers' silver gilt and enamel, officers' wire (worn on berets and introduced in 1951), officers' metal forage cap badges and black painted, anodized badges for wear in the field. Soldiers are also encouraged to purchase traditional gilding metal badges and polish them to a rich shine. Regulations, however, demand that the central cross of St George must be visible and not worn away. (Incidentally, George V bestowed the designation 'Guardsman' rather than 'Private' on the regiment in November 1918 in recognition of the sterling service of the Guards Division during the Great War, and another fascinating fact is that their motto *Nulli Secundis* dates from 1661 when, after being accepted as Household troops, Monk's Regiment of Foot was known as The Lord General's Regiment of Foot Guards when a Royal Commission designated them 'the second senior regiment of Household troops' – the first being the Grenadier Guards; somewhat peeved by what they thought was an unfair classification they decided upon their motto – *Second to None*.)

The cap badge of the Scots Guards features the star of the Order of the Thistle. Although recruits are issued with silver anodized versions of this badge, experienced soldiers are encouraged to purchase gilding metal versions that can be polished to a rich shine. The badge of officers and senior NCOs is a combination of a silver finish surrounding a gilded centre (that of officers being silver, gilt and enamel for wear on forage and service dress caps). Since 1944 1in × 2in patches of Royal Stuart tartan have been worn as a backing to Scots Guards beret badges (in fact, as early as 1916, officers of the 1st Battalion began to apply this tartan to either side of their service dress caps).

Raised in 1900, the Irish Guards wear a cap badge sporting the Star of the Order of St Patrick with the iconic shamrock leaf at its centre. As with the other foot regiments of the Household Division, versions of this badge differ depending on rank, ranging from anodized gilt versions through to bimetal badges for NCOs and silver, gilt and enamel versions for officers' service dress and forage caps and the colourfully elaborate officers' wire beret badge.

As did their forefathers who served with the Black Prince in 1314, men of the Welsh Guards wear a badge featuring the leek, ancient emblem of Wales. Welsh Guards have worn this badge since their formation in 1915 and up until the introduction of anodized badges in the 1950s this badge was made of brass. Trained soldiers and warrant officers generally wear privately purchased gilding metal cap badges, capable of being burnished. Officers wear wire-embroidered badges on all their caps. The embroidered cloth soldiers' khaki beret badge sits on a square of Household Division silk.

Not so long ago, the most senior regiment of line in the Army, The Royal Scots (The Royal Regiment), wore a cap badge introduced in 1986. It was based on the star of the Order of the Thistle and featured the patron saint of Scotland, St Andrew and the distinctive shape of the saltire upon which legend says he was crucified. However, in 2006 The Royal Scots were amalgamated with the King's Own Scottish Borderers to become the 1st Battalion of the new Royal Regiment of Scotland.

The new cap badge of this regiment incorporates details from the famous Scottish regiments from which it was formed, including the saltire device from The Royal Scots badge in recognition of their prime position in the British line. The cap badge of the Royal Regiment of Scotland also features the lion rampant and the motto *Nemo Me Impune Lacessit* ('No one wounds me with impunity').

Returning to the badge of The Royal Scots, collectors should know that during the period 1958–69 soldiers wore the Lowland Brigade cap badge – the regimental badge was worn on the collar. In 1969 junior ranks wore an anodized aluminium cap badge backed by red cloth visible through the voided piercing surrounding St Andrew and the saltire. Senior NCOs and officers wore variations of the silver staff badge bearing a gilded thistle at the centre.

The Tam O'Shanter beret badge of the Royal Scots differed for officers, senior NCOs and other ranks. Officers and NCOs wore a silver metal badge sitting above a square of Hunting Stewart tartan; other ranks wore only the square of tartan.

The Second Regiment of Line is also part of a much larger formation and again the result of amalgamations.

The Princess of Wales's Royal Regiment (PWRR) was formed in 1992, the result of the amalgamation of The Queen's Regiment with the Royal Hampshire Regiment.

Cap badge of The Royal Sussex Regiment, the regiment's first battalion was raised in 1702 as Ponsonby's Regiment. The Royal Sussex has the distinction of being the first regiment in the Army to march right across the continent of India.

BELOW RIGHT: Quite rare First World War cap badge of the Royal East Surrey Regiment.

The cap badge of the PWRR is also an amalgamation of elements from the badges of the two regiments from which it was formed, and their badges in turn were a mixture of devices from famous regiments including The Queen's Own Buffs (Tudor dragon), the Royal Hampshire Regiment (Hampshire rose) and the Royal Sussex Regiment (the surrounding garter awarded to the regiment in 1832).

The PWRR also incorporates the 2nd (The Queen's Royal) Regiment of Foot, awarded the title in 1751 when regimental numbering was introduced in Britain. Previously the 2nd of Foot, raised in 1661, were known as 'The Tangier Regiment' following their duties guarding a new British acquisition, the port of Tangier, part of Queen Catherine's dowry when she married Charles II. In 1881 the regiment's title was changed to The Queen's (Royal West Surrey Regiment). In 1959 the regiment amalgamated with the East Surreys, becoming The Queen's Royal Surrey Regiment.

The central and most distinctive feature of this famous regiment's cap badge was the paschal lamb –

a symbolic reference to the lamb of God, sacrificed like the lamb that was ceremonially eaten during Passover.

Silvered metal Buffs' cap badge, to be worn only by officers or senior NCOs.

In 1966 the regiment was one of the several Home Counties regiments amalgamated to form The Queen's Regiment, finally being absorbed into The Princess of Wales's Royal Regiment in 1992 as the result of yet more defence cuts.

Wartime economy Bakelite badge of the Middlesex Regiment.

Returning to the theme of the friendly rivalry between regiments according to their place in the order of precedence, I must now mention the 3rd Regiment of Foot, my father's old regiment The Buffs. 'Old Buffs' can trace their regiment's origins back to 1572, when they were raised for service in Holland as Thomas Morgan's Company. (My father attended the four hundredth anniversary celebrations of the regiment in 1972, by which time ex-Buffs who were still in the Army were then part of the new 'Queen's Regiment'.) Upon their return to England in 1665 they were renamed The Holland Regiment to commemorate the period of nearly a century they had passed in Dutch service.

It was not until 1751 that the title 3rd Regiment of Foot, or The Buffs, was officially sanctioned. Thirty years later they were affiliated to a county and renamed the 3rd (The East Kent) Regiment of Foot. The major changes instituted during the reforms of 1881 saw the regiment renamed The Buffs (East Kent Regiment), which they retained until their amalgamation with their county rivals The Queen's Own Royal West Kent Regiment, becoming The Queen's Own Buffs, The Royal Kent Regiment'.

RIGHT: **Cap badge of the Queen's Own Royal West Kent Regiment (1898–1961).**

BELOW: **Anodized cap badge of The Queen's Regiment. The dragon at the centre of the design is a legacy from the Buffs' badge, The Queen's Own Buffs being one of the regiments from the Home Counties Brigade, which formed the regiment in 1966 (the others being The Queen's Royal Surrey Regiment, the Royal Sussex Regiment and the Middlesex Regiment).**

BELOW RIGHT: **Cap badge of The Buffs (the Royal East Kent Regiment). This is an example of an old badge being found in very good condition. Too much cleaning would soon remove the dragon's scales.**

Until their absorption into the Queen's Regiment in 1966 the Buffs' cap badge prominently featured the regiment's Tudor dragon, the only major alteration to the design being the addition of 'Queen's Own' when the regiment amalgamated with The Queen's Own Royal West Kent Regiment in 1961, becoming the Queen's Own Buffs, The Royal Kent Regiment. The Buffs' dragon took precedence over the West Kent's white horse, Invicta, the ancient white horse of Kent and supposedly the burial marker of Horsa who, with his brother Hengist, led the Anglo-Saxon settlement of England.

With its diamond red backing, a feature of The King's Own Regiment's badge introduced in 1901, the badge of The King's Own Royal Border Regiment (the only infantry regiment in the Army that recruits exclusively from north Lancashire and Cumbria) dates from 1959 and the amalgamation of The King's Own Royal Regiment (Lancaster) and the Border Regiment.

Bimetal cap badge of the Middlesex Regiment, commemorating the honour won at the battle of Albuhera during the Peninsular War.

Queen's Own Buff's drummer's pouch badge; only twenty-five were ever produced.

BELOW: Vintage brochure from Canterbury's Buffs Regimental Museum. The cover shows red-coated soldiers with facings (turn-backs) of buff.

The Border Regiment cap badge (King's crown). The Regiment's many battle honours are inscribed on a Maltese cross. The surrounding laurel wreath commemorates the Regiment's chief battle honour won at Fontenoy in 1745.

The central lion of England is another feature retained from the earlier King's Own component. Tradition has it that William III bestowed this honour on the regiment because it was the first one to join his cause when he landed at Torbay in 1688.

In 1950 the Border Regiment was awarded the glider badge in recognition of the 1st Battalion's involvement in the first British glider landing, on Sicily in 1943. This, however, is worn only as an arm badge.

Featuring a flaming grenade similar to that of the Guards, the badge of the Royal Regiment of Fusiliers was formalized on St George's Day in 1968 with the amalgamation of the fusilier regiments of England, then serving together in the Fusilier Brigade. This distinctive bimetal anodized badge combines St George and the dragon from the cap badge of the Royal Northumberland Fusiliers, the crown from the badge of the Royal Fusiliers and the laurel wreath from the Lancashire Fusiliers. The Royal Warwickshire Fusiliers, another element within the Royal Regiment, are represented on the regiment's button. When worn on the beret, the Fusiliers' badge is topped by a red and white hackle.

The silver Hanoverian horse at the centre of The King's Regiment cap badge was awarded to the original King's Regiment (Liverpool) by George I in recognition of the unit's action at the battle of Dunblane, fighting against the Jacobites. The other major element of this cap badge is taken from that of the Manchester Regiment, The Manchesters and The King's Regiment (Liverpool) having amalgamated in 1958.

With the lion of England centre stage: the badge of Lancaster's the King's Own Royal Regiment.

ABOVE: The Royal Fusiliers (City of London Regiment), for wear on the racoon skin headdress adopted by fusilier regiments after 1901 (King's crown – brass).

King's crown cap badge of the Royal Fusiliers.

BELOW: Bimetal badge of The King's Regiment (Liverpool) 1927–50.

ABOVE: White metal badge of the Northumberland Fusiliers: 20th, 21st, 22nd and 29th Battalions (Tyneside Scottish), First World War.

ABOVE: Alternative design to the earlier version shown in this chapter of The King's Regiment (Liverpool). This can trace its history back to Princess Anne of Denmark's Regiment, formed by James II in 1685.

LEFT: Bedfordshire and Hertfordshire Regiment cap badge. Raised in 1688, this regiment has been called variously the Buckinghamshire and Leicestershire Regiment and the 16th Bedfordshire Regiment. The designation shown on this cap badge was obtained in 1919.

BELOW: Territorial Infantry Regiment Cap Badge of the Hertfordshire Regiment. The antecedents of this regiment go back to 1861 but in 1961 it amalgamated with The Bedfordshire Regiment to become The Bedfordshire and Hertfordshire Regiment (TA).

However, collectors should note that from 1958 until 1969 the regiment wore the Lancastrian Brigade cap badge, displaying its regimental affiliations only on the collar.

Combining elements from each of the East Midlands and East Anglian regiments, which merged on 1 September 1964 to form it, the badge of the Royal Anglian Regiment features the star from the Bedfordshire and Hertfordshire's badge and a representation of Gibraltar Castle, a feature of the Suffolks', Northamptonshires' and the Essex Regiment's badge, all components of the Anglians. When worn on a khaki beret the badge is backed by a black square for officers and a black 'tombstone' (a rectangle with a curved top) for soldiers.

A graphic interpretation of Exeter Castle is the main feature of the Devonshire and Dorset Regiment formed in 1958, following the amalgamation of the Devonshire Regiment and the Dorset Regiment. This feature was taken from the Devonshires' original badge as was the motto, *Semper Fidelis* (Ever Faithful). The Dorsets', however, supplied the Sphinx sitting in front of the castle. This was a battle honour awarded to them in 1802 at the battle of Marabout in Egypt. In keeping with the general arrangements at the time between 1958 and 1969, the Devonshire and Dorsets' actually wore the Wessex Brigade badge on their cap, regimental affiliations being reserved for the collar.

ABOVE LEFT: Formed in 1661 from the garrison of Windsor Castle, the Royal Suffolk Regiment's cap badge features the emblem of Gibraltar Castle (with a tiny key below it), awarded to the regiment for its part in the siege of 1779–83.

ABOVE RIGHT: Bimetal cap badge of the Northamptonshire Regiment. This was raised in 1881 and amalgamated with the Royal Lincolnshire regiment in 1960 to form the 2nd East Anglian Regiment (Duchess of Gloucester's Own Royal Lincolnshire and Northamptonshire).

RIGHT: Rare badge of The Devonshire Regiment's 4th Territorial Battalion (1908–21).

BELOW: Bimetal cap badge of the Lincolnshire Regiment. Raised in 1685, the Sphinx was added to the badge in 1801 to commemorate their actions against Napoleon in Egypt.

No.2 Dress badges are of bimetal, anodized construction, with black versions for wear on combat dress. Officers wear two versions of a wire-embroidered badge – on a green background for the beret and against blue when worn on the forage cap.

Formed in 1968, the Light Infantry was a result of the amalgamation of the Somerset and Cornwall Light Infantry, The King's Own Yorkshire Light Infantry, The King's Shropshire Light Infantry and the Durham Light Infantry. Originally wearing green feathers in their hats during the American War of Independence, the

RIGHT: **White metal cap badge of The Duke of Cornwall's Light Infantry.**

BELOW: **Formed in 1685, this First World War white metal cap badge of the Somerset Light Infantry (Prince Albert's) bears the motto Jellalabad, awarded for the regiment's defence of the city during the First Afghan War, 1841–42.**

light infantry companies of six regiments stained these red in defiance of a rebel vow to avenge the British victory at the battle of Brandywine. The Light Companies challenged the rebel threat to offer no quarter by responding that they were quite ready and

King's crown badge of the Royal Devon Yeomanry.

White metal cap badge of the Durham Light Infantry (King's crown).

Bronze cap badge of a territorial battalion of the Durham Light Infantry (King's crown).

had even highlighted their insignia rather than conceal themselves. Despite losing the red backing for a period in the 1960s, by 1968 this distinction had returned and to this day beret and service cap badges are backed with red.

On 1 February 2007 a new regiment, The Rifles, was formed from the Devonshire and Dorset Light Infantry, the Light Infantry, the Royal Gloucestershire, Berkshire and Wiltshire Light Infantry and the Royal Green Jackets. The brand new cap badge, which is

Bimetal badge of The King's Shropshire Light Infantry, the first battalion of which was raised in 1755 and the second battalion in 1793.

Awarded the Chinese dragon for their service in China in the nineteenth century, the Royal Berkshire Regiment (Princess Charlotte of Wales's) was formed in 1881.

illustrated here, uses the famous Light Infantry bugle and continues the concept of Light Infantry. The combination of Light Infantry and Rifle Regiments was developed by Sir John Moore at the turn of the nineteenth century and put to good use in the Peninsula during the Napoleonic Wars.

Created in 1958 following the amalgamation of the West Yorkshire Regiment (The Prince of Wales's Own) and the East Yorkshire Regiment (Duke of York's Own), the cap badge of The Prince of Wales's Own Regiment of Yorkshire prominently features the white horse awarded to the 14th Foot, an earlier element of the West Yorkshire Regiment. The East Yorkshires (15th Foot) were present with Wolfe at the capture of Quebec in 1759. In his memory the collar badges of officers of the East Yorkshires are backed with black and a black line is evident on the regiment's stable belt.

The Green Howards' cap badge featured the Dannebrog (cross) of the Danish royal family. This honour was bestowed on the regiment in 1874 when Alexandra, daughter of the King of Denmark, became Princess of Wales. The Green Howards have always had a close relationship with Scandinavia; in 1975 Olav V of Norway permitted the regiment's champion company to be known as King Olav's Company and for it to wear a copy of his Royal Bodyguard's badge as a sleeve emblem.

In 2006 the Yorkshire Regiment was created, an amalgamation of the Green Howards, The Duke of Wellington's Regiment (West Riding) and The Prince of Wales's Own Regiment of Yorkshire. The new cap badge is similar to that of the old Duke of Wellington's Regiment, featuring the Duke's crest and motto (this is the only time a non-royal's heraldic device has been permitted on a British Army badge), centred with the white rose of Yorkshire.

The Royal Highland Fusiliers became the 2nd battalion in the new super regiment The Royal Regiment of Scotland in March 2006. However, the regiment still wears the flaming grenade, a legacy of the Royal Scots Fusiliers, which amalgamated with the Highland Light Infantry in January 1959. Like all the other famous

ABOVE: **The Oxfordshire and Buckingham Light Infantry (43rd and 52nd) have one of the most illustrious records in the Army. During the prelude to D-Day in June 1944 the 52nd landed by glider at the bridges over the Caen Canal (Pegasus Bridge) and the River Orne (Horsa Bridge) and secured these vital places.**

RIGHT: **King's crown white metal First World War cap badge of The Yorkshire Regiment (Princess of Wales's Own).**

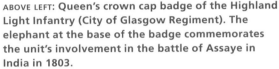

ABOVE LEFT: **Queen's crown cap badge of the Highland Light Infantry (City of Glasgow Regiment). The elephant at the base of the badge commemorates the unit's involvement in the battle of Assaye in India in 1803.**

ABOVE RIGHT: **The cap badge of The West Riding Regiment features the crest of the Duke of Wellington who was at one time the unit's commanding officer, hence its name The Duke of Wellington's Regiment; it was raised in 1702.**

RIGHT: **Mounted on regimental facings, a bimetal badge of the Nottinghamshire and Derbyshire Regiment (Sherwood Foresters) with the King's crown.**

regiments that amalgamated to form The Royal Regiment of Scotland, the Fusiliers' badge and tartan were retained by the pipes and drums of the regiment and, as do the other constituents, the Fusiliers wear their own distinctive hackle above The Royal Regiment of Scotland badge on their Tam O'Shanter.

Until 1922 the cap badge of the 22nd (Cheshire) Regiment featured a combination of an eight-pointed star and the encircling *Cheshire* motto in gilding metal with The Prince of Wales's feathers picked out in white metal. Apart from the period 1958–69 when the regiment wore the cap badge of the Mercian Brigade, the regiment's new badge consisted of a leaved acorn (said to commemorate an action by men of the regiment who saved George II from capture at the battle of Dettingen) in gold surrounded by a white (anodized) eight-pointed star.

The new reorganization of the army will see the Cheshires joining the Staffordshire Regiment, the Worcesters and the Sherwood Foresters in a new super regiment, the Mercian Regiment.

Raised in 1689, since its formation the Royal Welch Fusiliers have worn a cap badge representing a grenade, the traditional tool of their early craft, with the Prince of Wales's feathers. The grenade or bomb was traditionally of brass with the feathers picked out in white metal and both finishes were reproduced in anodized aluminium with the advent of Staybrite badges in the 1960s. In common with many other regiments, officers' versions of this badge were in

TOP: **King's crown cap badge of the 7th Battalion, the Sherwood Foresters ('The Robin Hoods').**

ABOVE: **Cap badge of the South Wales Borderers (24th Foot), one of the most famous regiments in the Army. They are perhaps most famous for their defence of Rorke's Drift in 1879, winning thirteen Victoria Crosses in doing so. In 1969 they were amalgamated with the Welch Regiment (41st/69th Foot) to form The Royal Regiment of Wales.**

TOP: **Bimetal cap badge of the Cheshire Regiment. The regiment was formed by the Duke of Norfolk in 1689 and the featured star with acorn and leaves is said to have been given to the regiment by George II.**

ABOVE: **King's crown cap badge of the 1st Battalion the Monmouthshire Regiment (1860–1971). During the First World War the regiment fielded eleven battalions and won battle honours for actions at Ypres, on the Somme and at Arras, Cambrai and Langemark. During the Second World War, as part of the Royal Artillery, the battalion was not eligible for battle honours.**

bronze metal. Combined, the Royal Welch Fusiliers and the Royal Regiment of Wales (formed in 1969 as the result of the amalgamation of the South Wales Borders and the Welch Regiment, whose cap badge since then simply bore The Prince of Wales's feathers and the motto *Ich Dien* (I Serve)) will comprise another new super regiment, the Royal Welsh.

With its famous badge showing Edinburgh Castle over St Andrew's cross, the design of The King's Own

Scottish Borderers' badge dates back to 1897. The badge sports two mottos: *Everything without the Lord is in vain* and *I trust in the truth of religion*. The KOSBs have

The King's Own Scottish Borderers badge, appropriately with the King's crown. The KOSBs were the local infantry battalion of the Borders.

Bimetal King's crown Irish Regiment of Canada cap badge bearing the motto *Fior go bas* (Gaelic for 'Faithful unto Death').

since been redesignated as The King's Own Scottish Borderers Battalion within the Royal Regiment of Scotland.

Appropriately enough, considering the losses of Irish soldiers during the First World War, the Royal Irish Regiment was formed on 1 July 1992, the seventy-sixth anniversary of the battle of the Somme. The regiment was the result of the amalgamation of the Royal Irish Rangers and the Ulster Defence Regiment. The new badge includes the harp and the crown from the Order of St Patrick, as instituted by George III in 1783 and a feature of Northern Irish regiments for most of the twentieth century. Rangers within the regiment wear a gold anodized aluminium badge on their green beret and a silver badge with a green hackle on their distinctive caubeen. Officers wear a wire-embroidered badge on their beret and a silver badge on the caubeen.

Since achieving fame in 1951 following their heroic stand on the River Imjin during the Korean War, the Gloucestershire Regiment, the 'Glorious Glosters', have undergone a variety of changes. The first since then was the award, unique in the British Army, of a US Army Presidential Unit Citation for their actions in Korea. This award was worn on both sleeves. In 1994 the Glosters amalgamated with The Duke of Edinburgh's Royal Regiment to form The Royal Gloucestershire, Berkshire and Wiltshire Regiment (RGBW). From 1994 the RGBW

wore a new badge featuring a white metal cross pattée centred with a gilded sphinx with *Egypt* beneath. The style of the cross pattée is based on the classic heraldic emblem traditionally worn by Teutonic knights.

This design of this short-lived cap badge (it was changed again in 2005 when its size was reduced) was a synthesis of the Wiltshire Regiment's cross, the Gloucestershire Regiment's sphinx and the red, Brandywine backing of the Royal Berkshire Regiment. On the back of their headdress the RGBW wore the famous back badge – The Royal Gloucesters' sphinx surrounded by laurels commemorating the time when as the 28th Regiment they fought back to back in Egypt in 1801.

The regiment converted to a light infantry unit in July 2005 and, before the formation of the Rifles, were titled the Royal Gloucestershire, Berkshire and Wiltshire Light Infantry. In 2007 they became part of a new super regiment, the Rifles (*see* above). Together with its light infantry bugle horn cap badge, the Rifles will continue the tradition dating back to the Royal Gloucestershire Regiment's time of wearing the famous back badge on its headdress.

Combining the garter star from the badge of the 29th Regiment of Foot, the Worcestershire Regiment, with the Maltese cross, oak wreath and stag of the Sherwood Foresters' badge, the new badge of the

The Nottinghamshire and Derbyshire Regiment can trace its development back to a battalion of marines in 1740. In 1881 it was known as The Sherwood Foresters (Derbyshire Regiment) and in 1902 Nottinghamshire was added to the regiment's title.

Worcestershire and Sherwood Foresters Regiment came into being in 1970. On 1 September 2007 the Worcestershire and Sherwood Foresters badge changed again, when the regiment joined with the Cheshire Regiment and the Staffordshire Regiment to create the Mercian Regiment. The new badge features a double-headed Mercian eagle beneath a Saxon crown.

The East Lancashire, South Lancashire and Loyal North Lancashire Regiments fought alongside each other during the South African War (1899–1902), The Loyal North Lancashires being awarded a battle honour for the defence of Kimberley, the siege of which was raised on 15 February 1900 – neatly at the beginning of the period considered by this book.

With the introduction of service dress, the regimental badges, which up to then had consisted of helmet plate centres (the East and the South Lancashires, for example, featuring a sphinx surrounded by the county designation, the Loyal North Lancashires, the Lancastrian rose surmounted by a crown), all changed to more 'modern' designs. These featured a combination of laurel wreaths, the Lancastrian rose and the emblem of the sphinx. The Royal North Lancashires featured only the Lancastrian rose.

Uniquely, the Glosters wore a *Back Badge* together with their famous cap badge. This tradition commemorates the regiment's actions in Alexandria in 1801. Then the 28th Foot (North Gloucestershire) under the command of General Sir Ralph Abercromby, they landed in Egypt against strong French opposition. At Alexandria a combined British force brought the French army to battle. The 28th took up a key defensive position defending the British flank but were soon cut off by the French onslaught. With no reserves available at this critical point in the battle, Lt Col Chambers, who had taken over command following the serious wounding of the CO, Col Paget, gave the historic order 'Rear rank, 28th! Right about face!'. The rear ranks turned and with exemplary discipline waited until the French cavalry were a few horse lengths away. The combined ranks stood firm unleashing a devastating volley from their muskets that caused such heavy casualties amongst the cavalry that they were forced to withdraw. For the gallantry in fighting back to back, the Regiment was given the unique honour of wearing a badge on the rear of their caps. This honour has prevailed. Back Badge day is celebrated on 21 March each year. On 1 February 2007 the Royal Gloucestershire, Berkshire and Wiltshire Light Infantry merged with the Devon and Dorset Light Infantry to become 1 Rifles. The regular battalions of the Rifles will wear the Back Badge with ceremonial dress, and officers and warrant officers will also wear it on side hats.

Bimetal other ranks' badge of the Lancashire
Fusiliers, worn until 1921.

In 1958 the East and the South Lancashire Regiments
amalgamated to form the Lancashire Regiment (Prince
of Wales's Volunteers) and in 1970 The Loyal North Lancashire Regiment joined them. The regiment's new
anodized aluminium badge featured a large Lancastrian
Rose surmounted by a crown and with the words
'Queen's Lancashire' in a scroll beneath it. Soldiers had
to paint the petals of the anodized badge red until it was
replaced by a gilt and enamel version in 2003.

On 1 July 2006 The Queen's Lancashire Regiment
amalgamated with The King's Own Border Regiment
(whose cap badge featured the lion of England within a
laurel leaf surmounted by the monarch's crown) and
The King's Regiment (whose cap badge was a combination of the Manchester Regiment's fleur-de-lis and
white horse of Hanover from The King's Liverpool's
badge, the two regiments having amalgamated in
1958) to form another new super regiment, The Duke
of Lancaster's Regiment (King's, Lancashire and Border).

The new badge of The Duke of Lancaster's Regiment proudly bears a central Lancastrian rose, laurel
wreath and the motto *Nec Aspera Terrent* (Frightened
by No Difficulties, or Difficulties Be Damned).

The next regiment in the traditional order of precedence, the Staffordshire Regiment, whose cap badge
always featured the Prince of Wales's plumes above
the famous Stafford knot – the origins of which are
unknown – is now part of the new Mercian Regiment.

The famous 'Ladies from Hell', the fearless soldiers of
The Black Watch (The Royal Highland Regiment) have
long had the rare distinction among soldiers wearing
cap badges in the Army of *not* having to wear one,
instead, they wore only a red hackle in place of a cap
badge. The regimental badge was either of bimetal, silver and gilt (for officers) or anodized aluminium construction and featured a combination of the Star of the
Order of the Thistle with a central depiction of St

First World War King's crown badge of the Border
Regiment.

Second World War (King's crown) cap badge of the
South Staffordshire Regiment, featuring the Stafford
knot, one of the devices of the Lords of Stafford.

ABOVE LEFT: **King's crown badge of the Black Watch (The Royal Highlanders) – the senior Highland regiment.**

ABOVE: **Second World War Royal Highlanders' (Black Watch) badge to be worn on the glengarry. During the twentieth century regular battalions generally declined to wear this in the field, preferring the red feather hackle on their Tam-O'-Shanters.**

BELOW: **In 1793, led by Sir Alan Cameron of Erracht, the Cameron clan formed The Queen's Own Cameron Highlanders (white metal cap badge).**

Andrew and the saltire and was worn on the glengarry, mess dress and by pipers. Now redesignated as the Black Watch, 3rd Battalion The Royal Regiment of Scotland (3 Scots), it wears its famous red hackle along with the new super regiment's badge.

The Highlanders, now 4 Scots within The Royal Regiment of Scotland, were formed in 1994, following the amalgamation of two famous Scottish regiments, The Queen's Own Highlanders (Seaforth and Cameron) and the Gordon Highlanders. The new regiment's badge was that of The Queen's Own Highlanders. The Seaforth Highlanders had worn this distinctive combination of crowned thistle, stag's head and scrolled motto since the eighteenth century. Legend has it that, in 1266, Colin Fitzgerald of Kintail prevented a stag from goring Alexander III of Scotland who had been unhorsed during the hunt. Shouting 'Cuidrch'n righ' ('Help the king'), the motto on the Highlanders' badge, he despatched the stag with a single sword blow.

Despite wearing The Queen's Own Highlanders' badge in favour of the Gordons', the unit wore the Gordon Highlanders' kilt.

The Argyll and Sutherland Highlanders (Princess Louise's) now constitute the 5th Battalion of The Royal Regiment of Scotland (5 Scots). Adopted in 1881, until its partial subordination to the new Royal

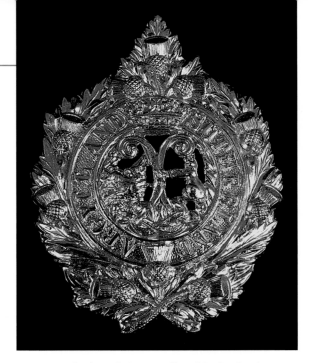

ABOVE: **Cap badge of the Argyll and Sutherland Highlanders (Princess Louise's) formed from the merger of the two Highland regiments in 1881.**

ABOVE RIGHT: **Anodized Staybrite cap badge of the Parachute Regiment; after 1953, hence the Queen's crown.**

Plastic Second World War economy version of the Argyll and Sutherlands' badge.

Regiment of Scotland's one, the Argyll and Sutherlands' cap badge was the largest and also the oldest badge in the Army. This elaborate design changed little during the twentieth century. Sometimes the central design of the badge was voided, sometimes the tail of the wildcat to the right of the boar's head changed in style, but it always incorporated a wreath of myrtle entwined with a wreath of butcher's broom, at the centre of which was the monogram of Princess Louise. Officers wore a silver badge and other ranks could opt for old or newly produced white metal versions or wear the standard anodized aluminium one.

Formed in 1942, the Parachute Regiment first received their cap badge in 1943 and since then it has not altered in design other than the change from the King's to the Queen's crown in the mid 1950s. The clas-

White metal badge of the Cameronians (Scottish Rifles). The only rifle regiment in the Scottish infantry, they were formed in 1881, the result of one of the many amalgamations recommended by the review of the Army.

sic design of outstretched wings surrounding a central parachute harks back to the embroidered blue and white emblem worn by qualified Army parachutists, introduced in 1940. Until the anodized badge was introduced in 1958, both King's and Queen's crown versions were manufactured from white metal. In the 1970s a black metal version was introduced for wear on active service in Northern Ireland. On occasions personnel in Parachute Regiment training units wear these black badges. Officers wore silver wings on their red berets, but in recent years new white metal badges have been manufactured, a great improvement over the anodized aluminium versions and are now worn by all ranks.

The Gurkhas

At the end of the Nepalese war in 1816, the British encouraged Nepalese soldiers to join the ranks of the East India Company. When the Company was abolished, following the Indian Mutiny in 1858, its Gurkha regiments were transferred to the British Indian Army. At the start of the Great War ten Gurkha regiments fought in numerous theatres. Further battalions were formed and during both world wars some 200,000 of these tough mountain men fought for the British.

Indian independence in 1947 saw a tripartite agreement between India, Nepal and Britain that enabled four regiments of Gurkhas, each of two battalions, to remain in the British Army. Consequently, the 1st and 2nd Battalions of the 2nd, 6th, 7th and 10th Gurkhas transferred to the British Army. The Brigade of Gurkhas was thus formed. The design of the badges of each regiment within the Brigade featured crossed kukris, the traditional Gurkha fighting knife.

Until the amalgamation of the regiments into the Royal Gurkha Rifles (see below), collectable badges were many and varied and included the 2nd King Edward VII's Own Gurkha Rifles (The Sirmoor Rifles) officers' silver-plate forage and field service cap badge, featuring The Prince of Wales's plumes, coronet and motto; the cap badge of the 10th, Prince Mary's Own Gurkha Rifles, featuring a rather elaborate design of a bugle-horn and strings interlaced with a kukri, its edge

Surmounted by an Imperial King's Crown (Edward VII), this cap badge of the celebrated 3rd Gurkha Rifles changed in 1907 when the unit became the 3rd The Queen's Own Gurkha Rifles in honour of Alexandra of Denmark, queen consort of the King. In 1908 their title became more specific – the 3rd Queen Alexandra's Own Gurkha Rifles. The unit was the last of the four Gurkha battalions raised in 1815 and was then known as the Kemaon Battalion. The battalion was to police the Nepalese border for forty years before their arduous march to Delhi and their assault on the Kashmir gate during the Mutiny of 1857. After the Mutiny, they were counted as one of the Bengal Line regiments – the 18th Regiment of Bengal Native Infantry – but in 1864 they became 3rd Goorkha (The Kemaon) Regiment, and engaged in the Afghan Wars, the Tirah campaign and along the Punjab Frontier. In the First World War, the 3rd won two VCs, one at Loos on the Western Front and the other in Palestine, where a detachment from the 3rd battalion served under Lawrence of Arabia.

facing downwards, manufactured in silver plate for officers and anodized silver aluminium for other ranks, and that of the 7th Duke of Edinburgh's Own Gurkha Rifles, which featured a pair of crossed kukris pointing upwards and surmounted by the Duke of Edinburgh's coronet and his cipher. Formed in 1994 after the amalgamation of the four Gurkha rifle regiments, the Royal Gurkha Rifles wear a cap badge of crossed kukris backed with a square of Hunting Stuart tartan.

Royal Green Jackets

As we have seen, the Royal Green Jackets, traditionally next in order of precedence, are now part of the new

The Artists Rifles was raised in 1859 as part of a widespread movement to increase Britain's volunteer reserve in case of French invasion. Patriotic artists, including Frederic Leighton, established it and the unit's first HQ was at Burlington House, the home of the Royal Academy. The badge was designed by William Wyon, Chief Engraver at the Royal Mint and also responsible for the earliest engravings of royalty on British postage stamps. The design he chose features the heads of the Roman gods Mars and Minerva in profile. In 1967, as 21st SAS, the Artists' Rifles became a reserve regiment in the Territorial Army.

super regiment The Rifles. However, it is worth taking a closer look at their famous badge and the regiments who amalgamated to form the Green Jackets in 1966.

When it was designed in 1966, the Royal Green Jackets' new badge was a synthesis of the traditional rifle and light infantry regiment's bugle horn with the Maltese cross from the former badges of The King's Royal Rifle Corps and the Rifle Brigade. At the base of the cross a naval crown commemorates the Rifle Brigade's involvement in the battle of Copenhagen in 1801. Issue anodized aluminium, nickel, officers' silver and even black plastic badges (introduced in 1989 to replace the previously black painted beret badges of the 3rd Battalion) were worn.

Special, Air and Naval Forces

Perhaps one of the most famous badges in the British Army is that of the Special Air Service (SAS). This unit was formed in 1941 by the legendary David Stirling and, together with the Long Range Desert Group, involved itself in causing mayhem behind Italian and later German lines. From the beginning it adopted its classic winged dagger badge. Apparently, the designer, Sgt Bob Tait, MM, actually based it on King Arthur's sword, Excalibur. However, as the stiletto-bladed Fairburn-Sykes fighting knives carried by the SAS and those of the Commandos looked similar and were well known by the North African tailors who embroidered the first badges in theatre, this interpretation of the famous weapon has stuck in the public's mind. Stirling himself thought of the motto 'Who Dares Wins', and the light and dark blue colours on the scroll and flames are said to be based on the rowing colours of Oxford and Cambridge.

The SAS first wore this badge on the khaki field service cap but quickly adopted a white beret. This then changed to beige. Immediately following the war the regiment was disbanded. When it was reformed in 1952 it wore a maroon beret, but in 1957 changed back to beige as it now remains.

The Special Boat Squadron (SBS) can trace its history back to 1940 when the Commandos established their special Folboat section. In 1942 this came under the auspices of the SAS, but when the Commando and SAS special marine units amalgamated it became a new Special Boat Squadron until the unit was disbanded in 1945. Today, the ethos of the original unit lives on in the Royal Marines' Special Boat Service, whose badge is very similar to that of the SAS, sharing the depiction of Excalibur, but with the addition of water and the letters SBS.

Formed in 1941 on the insistence of Winston Churchill, who, like so many observers at the time, had been impressed by the *Wehrmacht*'s deployment of glider-borne troops during the invasion of Belgium and the Low Countries, The Glider Pilot Regiment wore their distinctive white metal cap badge (an eagle surrounded by the regimental title and surmounted by the monarch's crown) until 1957. In 1957 the Glider Pilot Regiment's Light Liaison Flights joined with RAF Air Observation Post Squadrons to form a new unit, the Army Air Corps.

The Army Air Corps cap badge is almost identical to the old Glider Pilot Regiment one. This anodized aluminium badge is worn on a Cambridge blue beret, backed by a square of dark blue felt. Officers wear a wire-embroidered badge on their beret. The current Army Air Corps is not the British Army's first involvement with flying. The Royal Air Force can trace its history back to the Army's Royal Engineers and Royal Flying Corps (*see below*) and the original Army Air Corps (formed in 1942) comprised the Glider Pilot Regiment, the Parachute Battalions (later the Parachute Regiment) and the Air Observation Post (AOP) Squadrons, which flew light aircraft and spotted for the guns.

No discussion of the seismic changes in the technological development of the British Army in the early twentieth century would be complete without mention of the Royal Flying Corps. Formed in response to a Royal Warrant issued in May 1912, the RFC superseded the Air Battalion of the Royal Engineers and added aeroplanes to the Army's inventory of modern weapons.

For six years, until the creation of an independent air arm in 1918 (the Royal air Force), reconnaissance, combat fighter patrols and the bombing of enemy troop dispositions were the province of the RFC and the Royal Navy's air component, the Royal Naval Air Service (RNAS). Soldiers and sailors were the only service personnel to wear wings on their tunics. The RNAS was formed in 1914, two years after the RFC, because the Navy successfully lobbied for its own air component independent from Army control. Although both ceased to exist with the creation of the RAF, the Navy once again argued for its own air service and the Fleet Air Arm was established in 1939.

Mention is made here of the RNAS, because like the Machine Gun Corps and the RFC, particular examples of its badges are featured here. Its main relevance to a book about Army badges is its despatch to Ostend in August 1914 in support of the Belgium Army. While there, its commanding officer gathered together motor vehicles for use as reconnaissance vehicles. Soon armour in the shape of individual pieces of boilerplate was added to these civilian vehicles and the first military armoured cars were born.

ABOVE: Cap badge of the Glider Pilot Regiment (King's crown) – this is quite rare. This unit was formed in 1941 and was disbanded in 1957. Formed partly in response to the apparent successes of German glider-borne troops in 1940, the regiment earned its laurels on D-Day when Allied glider pilots manoeuvred their often overladen Horsa and Hamilcar gliders close to key coastal defences.

BELOW: Cap badge of the Royal Flying Corps. It only ever featured a King's crown because at the end of the First World War the Army relinquished control of military flying and the Royal Air Force was born.

ABOVE: **First World War RN infantry Nelson Battalion badge.**

BELOW: **First World War RN Armoured Car Squadron cap badge.**

This book includes examples of many of the First World War units mentioned above, including an example of the badge of the Royal Naval Division's Nelson Battalion (one of eight infantry battalions, each named after a famous admiral). In fact, because the Royal Navy had not been involved in any major ship-to-ship actions since 1850, by 1914 it had become accepted practice that the Royal Marines and seamen would support the Army on land as they had done during the Crimean War, the Indian Mutiny, the Boxer Rebellion in China and the Boer War, where the most famous engagement in which the Naval Brigade was involved took place during the Relief of Ladysmith in 1899.

Supporting Services

It is beyond the scope of this work to look in detail at the badges of every department and corps of the British Army, but some are well known and illustrated here. One of the most famous is that of the Royal Electrical and Mechanical Engineers (REME) who were formed in 1942 from men of the Royal Army Ordnance Corps (RAOC), the Royal Engineers (RE) and the Royal Army Service Corps (RASC). REME's badge changed from the original one featuring four laurel-surrounded shields each bearing a letter from the corps' title, with a pair of callipers at the centre, to the rather more dramatic lightning flash in gilding metal with a chained white horse (suggesting horsepower under control) and coronet, introduced in 1947. Today, this design survives but in gilt and silver anodized aluminium.

The badge of the Royal Army Medical Corps (RAMC), featuring a serpent entwined around the rod of Aesculapius, the Greek God of medicine, is a traditional medical symbol and has been used since the cap badge was authorized in 1902. The motto *Steadfast in Adversity* was added in 1948 and a cherry red backing, included when the badge is worn on the beret, was added in 1956.

Initially bearing the words Military Police on a scroll at the bottom of a laurel wreath within which was the monarch's cipher, surmounted by the crown, the badge of the Military Police was introduced in 1908 in brass. In 1948 the force's title was changed to Royal Military

Police and was produced in gilding metal. In 1955 the Queen's crown was added and the cipher changed to EIIR; in 1958 the first anodized aluminium badges were produced. Officers' cap badges are manufactured from silver and their beret badges from embroidered wire.

Before its formation in 1914, the Army gathered military intelligence on a purely ad hoc basis when the need arose. Despite the Army being imbued with the teachings of many famous commanders, it was not until 1940 and the publication of Army Order 112 that the Intelligence Corps was formed.

I Corps' cap badge depicts a rose, the flower of secrecy, surrounded by laurel leaves. Although this was introduced in 1940, because they operated incognito, members of I Corps generally wore the insignia of the General Service Corps (during the Great War staff selected by the War Office for intelligence duties wore the badge of the Royal Fusiliers, operating behind the title of the 20th Battalion of that regiment).

The Intelligence Corps' motto *Manui Dat Cognitio Vires* (Knowledge Gives Strength to the Arm), was formally approved by Queen Elizabeth II in 1964. In 1985 the Corps' status was raised when it was officially

ABOVE: **During the Second World War, to save precious resources such as brass, many badges were produced in Bakelite, one of the oldest plastics. This King's crown badge belongs to the Royal Army Service Corps (RASC).**

BELOW: **Formed as result of Army Order 114, 1906, the Military Provost Staff Corps (previously named the Military Prison Staff Corps) was responsible for the imprisonment of unruly soldiers either in detention barracks (largely for rehabilitation) or in military prisons for those who had committed more serious crimes. This cap badge bears George V's King's crown.**

The Royal Corps of Signals (King's crown) was formed on 28 June 1920, a direct descendant of the Royal Engineers Signal Service of Great War fame.

Second World War vintage King's crown cap badge of the Intelligence Corps. Note that this badge has not been cleaned, the green deposits are harmless. *See* the text for advice on how to clean more serious deposits. In general, it is always better to leave the patina on old badges. Cleaning them to a bright shine will only remove further metal, losing relief in the crown and especially from the regimental title.

ABOVE: **Pre-1947 Palestine Police Force cap badge. I have included it here because time and time again this badge is classified either as a Jewish Brigade cap badge, in which case it would feature the 'Menorah', the traditional Jewish candlestick, or as belonging to the Jewish Chaplains' department, in which case it would feature a pierced design.**

BELOW: **The School of Musketry King's crown cap badge (worn 1902–19).**

declared a 'combat arm' rather than being seen as a rear support service of the Army.

The badges of the other principal corps include those of the Royal Army Chaplains' Department (introduced in 1940, one for Christian chaplains and the other for Jewish); the badge of the Royal Logistical Corps (introduced in 1993 following the amalgamation of the Royal Corps of Transport, the RAOC, the Royal Pioneer Corps, the Army Catering Corps and the Royal Engineers Postal and Courier Service and incorporating specific devices – the crossed axes from the old Pioneer Corps badge, the Royal Engineers' garter, the star and wreath from the Royal Corps of Transport); the crossed swords of the Army Physical Training Corps; the unique three crowns of the Adjutant General's Corps' cap badge; the laurel-wreathed centaur (Chiron) of the Royal Army Veterinary Corps (the design of which dates from 1918); the crossed rifles of the Small Arms School Corps; the crowned Lyre of Corps of Army Music (formed in 1994 but with a

heritage that can be traced back to the Royal Military School of Music, whose cap badge was introduced in 1907); the General Service Corps badge simply bearing the Royal Arms and introduced in 1942 in brass but now produced in gilt, bronze and anodized aluminium; and the Dannenborg-cross-based badge of Queen Alexandra's Royal Army Nursing Corps.

I began this book with a quotation from W.G. Clifford's *Peeps at the British Army*. The great changes in the structure of Britain's militia were relatively recent when he was writing at the outbreak of the First World War:

> Quite recently, during the administration of Haldane, great changes took place, changes which transformed the Militia into the Special Reserve, and the Volunteers

ABOVE: **King's Crown cap badge of the Royal Army Pay Corps.**

BELOW: **Queen's crown cap badge of the Army physical training staff.**

into the Territorials. The underlying idea of these changes was to weld all the military forces of the country into a more effective whole, to knit the parts closer together, to make one great army instead of three different forces, whose military relationship to each other was not close and distinct enough for modern requirements. Enlistment became universal, the old Volunteers were enrolled, but the Territorials were duly attested as Regular soldiers are; and in many other respects a strenuous attempt was made to bring every soldier of the King in line, or as near in line as could be considering the amount of time the individual could spare for training.

Militia, Yeomanry and Territorials

One of the results of this was the creation of many new Yeomanry regiments. In fact, the major reorganization of the Army in 1908 saw the abolition of the nineteenth-century militia and the consolidation of the Yeomanry and the Volunteers into the new Territorial Force (which became the Territorial Army in 1920). The Yeomanry cavalry regiments kept their titles but the infantry went to join the regular battalions of their county infantry regiments, the 1st Volunteer Battalion of the East Yorkshire Regiment becoming its 4th Battalion, for example. The Great War had proved the futility of mounted battalions and most Yeomanry cavalry became either armoured car units or joined the artillery (one became a signals unit).

When the Territorial Army was reconstituted again in 1947, although most of the old Yeomanry regiments appeared under their old titles (other than The Middlesex Yeomanry, which formed part of the Royal Corps of Signals) they were either regiments within the Royal Armoured Corps or the Royal Artillery. Many of the badges of the surviving Yeomanry regiments are illustrated in this book.

Two of them, the North of Ireland Imperial Yeomanry along with the South of Ireland Imperial Yeomanry, were gazetted by Royal consent in January 1902.

Along with other famous Irish regiments such as the Royal Irish Regiment, the Royal Dublin Fusiliers and

ABOVE: **Rare Fife and Forfarshire Yeomanry (1908–22) cap badge in white metal.**

BELOW: **King's crown Territorial Army lapel badge enabling a member of the TA to display his national service when wearing civilian clothes.**

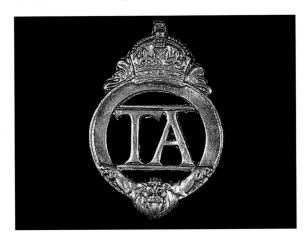

Staybrite cap badge of the South Nottinghamshire Hussars, now part of the 100th (Yeomanry) Field Regiment Royal Artillery.

the Connaught Rangers, the South Irish Horse were disbanded in 1922 with the establishment of the Irish Free State.

However, although temporarily disbanded in 1919, the North of Ireland Imperial Yeomanry, which had been renamed the North Irish Horse in 1908, continued to wear its famous badge of the Irish harp surmounted by the monarch's crown with the title North Irish Horse on a scroll beneath, when it was reformed in 1922, that

momentous year in Irish history. In 1939 the North Irish Horse was transferred from the Corps of Cavalry of the Line to the Royal Armoured Corps and designated a light armoured regiment of the supplementary reserve.

Today, four Yeomanry regiments proper survive to carry on the traditions of their volunteer predecessors. However, some modern Territorial Army (see below) artillery, engineer and signals units continue to use their former Yeomanry titles.

The Royal Yeomanry was created in 1967 from squadrons of the Berkshire and Westminster Dragoons, the Royal Wiltshire Yeomanry, the Sherwood Rangers Yeomanry, the Kent and County of London (Yeomanry) and the North Irish Horse. Each squadron was permitted to wear its own cap badge. Things changed again in 1992 when the Sherwood Rangers joined and the North Irish Horse became independent. Further reorganizations included the addition of the Leicestershire and Derbyshire Squadron and the Berkshire Squadron, formed as recently as 1995, transferring to the Royal Signals. Although Royal Yeomanry personnel wore the individual cap badges of their former regiment, they are bound together by a Royal Yeomanry Tactical Recognition Flash (TRF) worn on the right upper sleeve of their combat jackets. The colours of the Royal Yeomanry's TRF are based on the ribbon of the South African War Medal awarded in 1902 – the first to be awarded to volunteers.

ABOVE: Brass King's crown cap badge of the Connaught Rangers.

RIGHT: White metal King's crown cap badge of The Royal Ulster Rifles. Formed in 1913 as The Royal Irish Rifles, their name was changed in 1920; they were disbanded in 1952.

BELOW: Distinctive brass badge of the South Irish Horse. This unit lasted for only twenty years. It was raised as the South of Ireland Imperial Yeomanry in 1902 and disbanded along with other Irish regiments in 1922, consequently its badge is now rare and collectable.

BELOW RIGHT: Cap badge of the Royal Ulster Rifles, formed in 1881 by the amalgamation of the 83rd Foot (County of Dublin) Regiment and the 86th (Royal County Down) Regiment. Their badge featured the harp of Ireland combined with the British crown.

ABOVE: **Rare King's crown cap badge of the North Irish Horse.**

RIGHT: **First World War King's crown cap badge of The King's Liverpool Regiment (8th Scottish Volunteer Battalion).**

In 1971 the Royal Wessex Yeomanry was formed from elements of the Royal Wiltshire Yeomanry, the Royal Gloucestershire Yeomanry and the Royal Devon Yeomanry. Like the Royal Yeomanry, the Royal Wessex have no cap badge of their own, squadrons wear the badges of their historic affiliations thereby preserving unit traditions.

The Royal Mercian and Lancastrian Yeomanry united the Royal Mercian Yeomanry with The Duke of Lancaster's Own Yeomanry in 1992. They were given a badge that combined the Mercian Imperial Eagle with the Duke of Lancaster's rose and coronet, the eagle being picked out in silver against the red enamel of the rose, offset against a gilt coronet and crown. Officers wore a wire-embroidered version of this badge.

The Queen's Own Yeomanry was created in 1971. Their badge, a running fox, is based on the design of the old East Riding of Yorkshire Yeomanry. Soldiers' badges are produced in gold and silver anodized aluminium and those worn by officers are manufactured from silver and gilt. For both badges the fox is picked out in gold and the scrolled title in silver.

Today the Territorial Army (TA) is a massive supplement to the regular army. TA soldiers are issued only with combat dress; officers and senior NCOs also wear mess dress and a quantity of No.1 and No.2 Dress

uniforms are available for ceremonial use. Therefore the only cap badge generally worn is the beret badge, generally that of the local regiment to which the TA battalion is affiliated.

There are, however, some TA units with such a long tradition of volunteer service that they retain individual and highly collectable cap badges. Among these the most senior is that of the Royal Monmouthshire Royal Engineers (Militia), a unit that can trace its roots back to 1539. Featuring The Prince of Wales's feathers, their badge is based on the design of the nineteenth-century Royal Monmouthshire Militia.

No survey of the badges of famous TA regiments can be at all complete without mention of that of The Honourable Artillery Company (HAC). They wear three different badges: a silver grenade emblazoned with the HAC cipher (which can be also be worn painted black and is set against the Household Division's backing when worn on the unit's khaki beret), an embroidered beret badge bearing the arms of the City of London and a distinctive soldiers' beret badge (a silver winged arm grasping a sword). The HAC was formed in 1537 and performs a variety of ceremonial duties in London and has a close affiliation with the Royal Artillery (within which it is a TA regiment), even firing Royal salutes from the Tower of London.

Rare King's crown badge of The Duke of Connaught's Own Royal East Kent Yeomanry (Mounted Rifles).

The Hong Kong Volunteer Corps was established in the nineteenth century when Britain's commitments in the Crimea reduced the number of soldiers in the colony. The unit saw action during the Japanese invasion during December 1941 and surrendered on Christmas Day.

It is beyond the scope of this book to examine the badges of the numerous other volunteer and yeomanry units affiliated to the Royal Artillery, the Royal Engineers, the Royal Signals, infantry, REME, airborne and Special Forces, the Royal Army Medical Corps and the other services and corps. Neither is it my intention to examine units within the Officer Training Corps, Army Cadet Force, or the bands and pipers affiliated to regiments and corps. The collector can have fun researching all of these and the bibliography should prove a good place to start. However, no survey of volunteer forces is complete without mentioning the Home Guard.

Home Defence

The British people were in turmoil following the dramatic events of May 1940, when Hitler's forces swept into Belgium and the Low Countries. Allied plans depended on halting German troops along a river line in southern Belgium, up to which they would advance only at the latest possible time. What plans there were, fell to pieces as armoured forces threaded their way through the Ardennes, far from the assumed tactical theatre, effectively outflanking Anglo-French defences. Despite the fact that almost the entire professional British Army constituted the quarter of a million men of the British Expeditionary force (BEF) and were on the Continent, the new Prime Minister Winston Churchill began to give urgent thought to home defence. So did the public, and bands of unofficial militia were soon found to have armed themselves in preparation for a German invasion. Something had to be done, both to shore up the bulwarks of Britain's defence and to give morale a much-needed boost, and on 14 May the Secretary of State for War Anthony Eden broadcast a request for volunteers to join a new organization, the Local Defence Volunteers (LDV), to supplement the regular defences.

Within a month, nearly 750,000 men had joined the LDV (planners had forecast that around 150,000 might and consequently the organization was underfunded and disorganized in its early days). On 23 July the LDV was renamed the Home Guard, which Churchill thought more stirring and appropriate.

Although the LDV did not exist for long, a printed khaki brassard was produced and soon abandoned when the new Home Guard one was manufactured to replace it – this at a time when Britain stood alone. Although members of the Home Guard wore the cap badges of their county regiments together with their brassards, cloth shoulder titles and battalion/county codes worn on the shoulder below the words 'Home Guard', some units did have individual cap badges and these are now becoming increasingly rare. Among them and the most collectable are those of the Isle of Man force, which features the three legs of the Manx arms with the motto *Quocunque Jeceris Stabit* (Whichever way you throw me I will stand) and a circlet scroll inscribed Home Guard, and that of the Upper Thames Patrol (illustrated here) with overlapping escutcheons with the arms of the City of London and Thames Conservancy above a tablet with the letters UTP.

Formed during the invasion scare of 1940, the Auxiliary Units were a top-secret cadre of volunteers who had elected to join 'stay behind' patrols, ostensibly working under the auspices of the Home Guard but in reality commanded by a combination of GHQ Home Forces and the Department of Military Intelligence, which formed the world's first military resistance established before enemy occupation.

Auxiliary Units were established nationwide and consisted of three battalions – 201 covering Scotland and northern England, 202 the Midlands and 203 London and the southern counties.

The organization was run on a strictly 'need to know' basis and volunteers were encouraged to carry nothing at all that could identify them or their unit if they were captured. They wore standard Home Guard brassards, the cap badge of the county regiment to which their battalion was affiliated and standard county shoulder titles, together with the battalion number relating to the sector in which they operated. As the risk of an invasion became increasingly unlikely the running of the organization became more relaxed, so much so that the force commissioned its own discreet lapel badge – a red and blue GHQ shield bearing a battalion number emblazoned in a gold cross formation. Surviving examples of these badges, issued on only a highly limited basis, are very rare indeed. The Auxiliary Units were disbanded in 1944.

Selection of British Second World War home defence equipment arranged against a rare Home Guard flag. The flag belongs to 8th Battalion City of London Home Guard and was one of eight presented to battalions of 'J' Zone Home Guard on 11 June 1944 (8th and 35th City of London Battalions and 51st, 52nd, 53rd, 54th, 55th and 56th Essex Battalions). Among the other items shown are Home Guard uniforms and brassards, field service cap, a couple of entrenching tool handles converted to accept the bayonet for the new No.4 rifle and a 'Swift' target rifle. This weapon, a training aid, fired a pin into a paper target mounted at the end of the barrel, the pin pricks displayed the accuracy of fire.

A Second World War Royal Artillery captain and RSM inspect the barracks of enlisted gunners at a coastal battery. No matter about the war emergency, spit and polish still had to be adhered to.

PUTTING IT ALL TOGETHER: SHOULDER TITLES, COLLAR BADGES AND CLOTH INSIGNIA

Collar Badges

Cap badges are really the tip of the iceberg, so to speak, of a British soldier's insignia. Although the precise arrangement has changed from time to time, uniforms could be bedecked with collar badges ('collar dogs'), shoulder titles, chevrons for NCOs and epaulette 'pips' for officers to denote rank, together with a range of other insignia such as cloth skill-at-arms badges or those denoting arm-of-service, together

ABOVE: Great War British cloth insignia: the Suffolk Regiment embroidered slip-on is an economy measure introduced to replace existing brass shoulder titles. They were designed to be attached to tunic epaulettes, although it was not unknown for them to be stitched to the top of the sleeve. The 'bombers' qualification badge was awarded to personnel trained to be most effective in the offensive use of the standard British hand-grenade, the Mills bomb.

RIGHT: Selection of cap badges, collar badges and buttons of The Queen's Royal Regiment (West Surrey). The paschal lamb was the crest of Catherine of Braganza, wife of Charles II, after whom the regiment was named when it was raised in 1661.

with regimental coloured flashes, formation ('divisional') emblems and detachable brassards for wear on pullovers.

The first regulated colour shoulder titles made from cloth were introduced in the Army in 1900. They were designed to be worn on the newly issued, khaki service dress and its accompanying greatcoat. It should be noted, however, that this was a short-lived dress modification; in 1907 metal regimental shoulder titles replaced cloth ones. In 1874 metal badges worn on the collar were introduced for infantry regiments. However, only private soldiers and NCOs wore these; one of the reasons for their introduction was the disappearance of numbers and other motifs denoting regimental affiliation from tunic buttons. As the final

ABOVE: **Royal Field Artillery lieutenant, about 1916, clearly showing how conspicuous his rank insignia made him compared with the plain sleeves of other ranks.**

RIGHT: **Neatly showing how Army insignia work as a whole, wearing his 'Sam Browne' field equipment, a lieutenant in the Royal Field Artillery about 1916. Of note is the system then employed to denote officers below the rank of brigadier. The insignia are worn on his cuff and then highlighted with khaki chevron lace. However, by the time of the Somme offensive many infantry officers in the field had dispensed with these and showed their rank on the epaulette using metal pips or stars. This made them far less conspicuous to the enemy who had become used to using the previous more elaborate rank insignia as an aiming point.**

RIGHT: **Embroidered Second World War battledress blouse sleeve insignia of The Queen's Royal Regiment (West Surrey).**

BELOW: **Selection of British battledress cloth shoulder titles (embroidered and printed). Officially sanctioned for the entire Army in 1943, the differing colours were drawn from the existing coloured designations for the several branches of service (red for infantry, burgundy for the RAMC and red and yellow for armoured troops).**

quarter of the nineteenth century began the Army's general service (GS) pattern buttons were standardized and emblazoned with only the Royal Arms. As new and individual cap badge designs were approved, a General Order of June 1874 permitted those regiments in possession of new insignia to wear versions of them on the collar. Those regiments without a badge were directed to use an imperial crown device.

By 1900, because officers' badges of rank had moved from the collar to shoulder cords, almost every rank in the Army was wearing some form or another of regimental collar insignia. It will be no surprise to discover that there are firm rules regarding the location and orientation of collar badges. These are worth knowing, especially if a collector wishes to display a pair of them and is in a quandary about their correct position. Generally, metal badges must be fixed midway between the top and the bottom of the collar. The centre of the badge should be precisely 2in from the collar's opening. If animals or birds are depicted on collar badges then they normally face inwards, towards the opening of the collar. If bugles are represented then the opposing mouthpieces should also be at the collar's opening. Generally, cloth badges are worn on the sleeve on one or both arms, depending on regulations.

Especially during the Second World War and principally for wear on khaki drill garments, a variety of formation, unit and officers' rank badges were

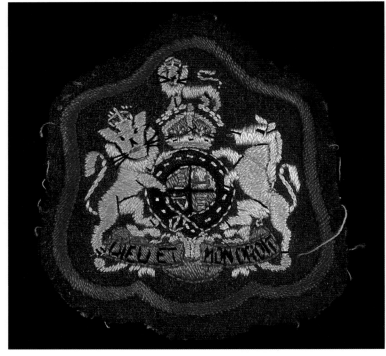

ABOVE: **Further selection of British cloth shoulder titles, including an authentic example from the Special Air Service Regiment.**

Second World War King's crown embroidered regimental sergeant major's badge of rank worn on the lower sleeve of service dress.

1970s' officer's slip-on rank insignia (captain) from 1st, 2nd or 3rd Battalion The Queen's Regiment. To be worn on the epaulettes of the famous 'woolly pully'.

Second World War Royal Tank Regiment tank crewman's sleeve insignia.

embroidered on to epaulette or shoulder-strap 'slides' or 'covers'. Although many cloth insignia are sewn direct on to a uniform, it is now increasingly the case that such insignia are attached to a removable brassard, thereby reducing the need for unit tailors to be forever transferring badges, especially those denoting rank, from one garment to another. This development also reduced the number of badges required for each soldier – an innovation no doubt greatly appreciated by the Treasury.

Some Special Badges

This book can only ever provide an overview of the types of cloth and metal insignia supplementary to the cap badge worn by the British soldier. However, I intend along the way to explore the cap badge's 'supporting cast', pointing out one or two special insignia. One cloth badge design featured here has early twentieth-century origins – the sleeve emblem of the Royal Tank Regiment. Selected personnel of the Heavy Branch of

ABOVE: **Formation sign of the 43rd (Wessex) Division.**

ABOVE RIGHT: **Rare Anti-Aircraft Command patch: first pattern (black design on dark red), the second pattern featured a somewhat more elaborate bow and a much brighter red.**

RIGHT: **Third pattern 4th Infantry Division Formation Sign.**

BELOW: **Formation emblem of HQ, Land Forces, Hong Kong, bearing the Chinese dragon rampant.**

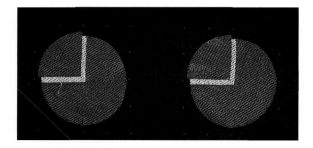

Battle patch of the British
1st Airborne Division as
worn on Dennison jump
smocks. It features
Bellerophon astride
Pegasus.

the Machine Gun Corps were equipped with tanks in 1917. They were permitted to wear Col Swinton's badge design embroidered on their upper right sleeve. Swinton was the visionary who conceived the notion of armoured fighting vehicles while serving in the Boer War. It featured the distinctive rhomboid profile of the original 'male' (equipped with sponson-mounted 6-pounders) and 'female' (machine gun) tanks. The metal cap badge (also based on Swinton's design) was not issued to the Regiment until 1922 by which time the newly designated Tank Corps was firmly established.

Another distinctive cloth badge featured shown here belongs to the Anti-Aircraft Command. Britain's air defences were proven woefully inadequate during the First World War, when even slow moving German Zeppelins roamed overhead more or less at will. With great prescience, AA Command was formed in April 1939, before Britain declared war on Germany on 3 September 1939.

Two patterns exist of the distinctive black-on-red upturned archer's long bow – the second bow being more elaborate than that featured on the first design.

An interesting development of a dragon, a common element in the design of many Army badges, is the stylized yellow 'Chinese' dragon on the red and black cloth patch of the HQ, Land Forces, Hong Kong.

An equally striking and perhaps more evocative emblem given its association with major campaigns such Arnhem is the 1st Airborne Division's formation patch featuring Bellerophon (hero of Greek mythology who slew the mighty Chimera) astride Pegasus, the winged horse. A version of this patch was embroidered on the Denison smocks worn by paratroopers of the division when they dropped in Holland in 1944.

Another distinctive and historic patch featured here is that of the 21st Signals Regiment (Air Support). It shows the outline of a red Beaufighter aircraft against a representation of sky, sea and land (to suggest the close cooperation between the unit and the RAF stations with which it liaised) and was introduced in 1948 (the regiment was formed in 1943).

Formed in 1920, the Royal Corps of Signals was created to supplement the Royal Engineer Signal Service, which until then had provided all ground communications other than wireless for the Army and, crucially, for the Air Force in overseas theatres. As it became obvious that the requirements of the RAF in this area would be enormous and that to coordinate Army/Air Force communications would become increasingly important, two regiment-sized units within the Royal Corps of Signals (Air Formation Signals 1 and 2) were formed and were among the first British troops to go to France in 1939. In 1959 the AFS regiments were merged into 21st and 22nd Signals Regiments. With the responsibility of providing communications systems for the RAF's Support Helicopter Force (SHF), currently only 21st Signals remains.

Another interesting fabric badge featured here depicts the yellow portcullis against a red cross on a white ground of the famous Home Counties Brigade. This formation, the 145th Infantry Brigade, was formed in 1908 and fought hard in both world wars.

It was disbanded in 1945 but reformed in 1995; as recently as 2004 its Brigade emblem was redesigned – the portcullis and cross of St George were replaced by a blue roebuck on a red diamond.

The red circle and *Berlin* on a dark blue background are reminders of the Cold War; they appear on a patch, the second pattern emblem for British troops stationed in the divided city until its reunification in 1990.

A wide range of skill-at-arms and qualification badges exists within the Army. The badge shown opposite featuring crossed white rifles against a khaki

ABOVE: **Air Formation Signals patch (*see* text).**

LEFT: **Second World War formation emblem of GHQ Home Forces.**

BELOW: **Emblem of an operational qualified paratrooper, the Parachute Regiment.**

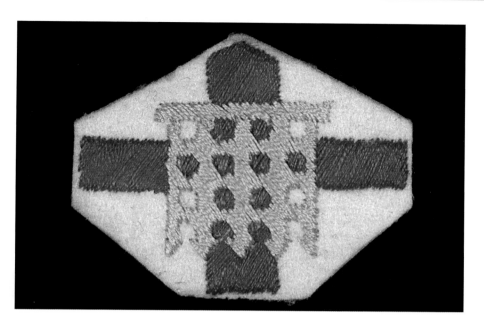

Home Counties Brigade formation patch.

Three skill-at-arms badges: two denoting a marksman (the red-backed example for wear on mess kit) and the crossed SMLEs, the badge of either a musketry instructor or a weapons training instructor.

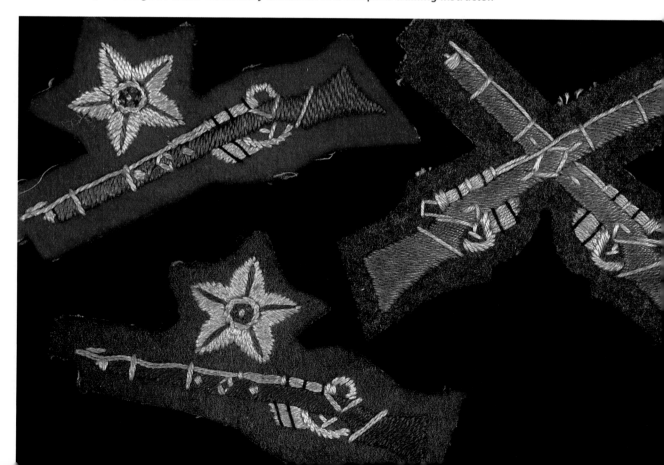

ABOVE: **Post-Second World War second pattern formation sign for British troops stationed in Berlin.**

BELOW: **The famous 'flaming a–hole' of a Royal Army Ordnance Corps ammunition technician or assistant ammunition examiner.**

background, is that of a Second World War weapons training instructor, rifle marksman. The Small Arms School Corps (SASC) is responsible for maintaining the proficiency of rifle and pistol shooting in the Army. It also has responsibilities for range management, helping to regulate the optimum ranges of service weapons and ensuring that soldiers can shoot accurately over such distances. The Small Arms School came into being in 1929, although the Corps can trace its origins back to the nineteenth century and the transition from smooth bore muzzle-loaders to carbines. It celebrated its centenary in 1953, and moved from Kent to Warminster in 1969, where it remains.

Looking vaguely reminiscent of a US airborne emblem, the flaming 'A' of a Royal Army Ordnance Corps ammunition technician/assistant ammunition examiner was introduced in cloth in 1949. Known colloquially by those who served the formation as the 'flaming a– hole' it replaced an earlier metal version.

Established during the Crimean War when Sir Colin Campbell united several Scottish regiments and formed the 51st Highland Brigade, this famous unit, by now a territorial division, mobilised for war in an amazing six days in 1914. Moving to France in 1915, the regiment was distraught to discover that their unit number, by now the 1st Highland Division, had been changed to the 51st. Despite this the formation ended

Formation sign of the 51st (Highland) Infantry Division.

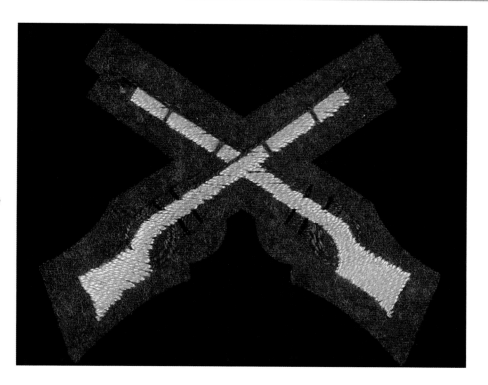

Sleeve emblem of a British weapons training instructor, rifle marksman.

the war with the reputation of being perhaps the hardest fighting unit in the British Army.

Sent to France again in 1939, the 51st Highland Division fought a legendary rearguard action, but were cut off at St Valery and could not be evacuated during Operation *Dynamo* along with the other 300,000 allied troops stranded in France. The formation's duplicate division (the 9th (Highland) Division)

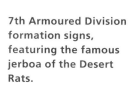

7th Armoured Division formation signs, featuring the famous jerboa of the Desert Rats.

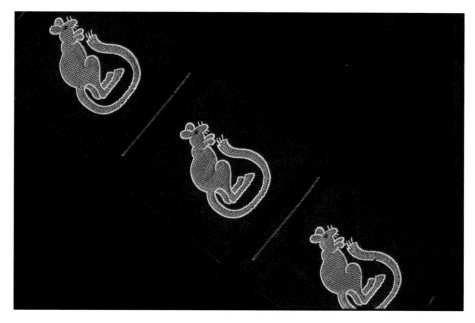

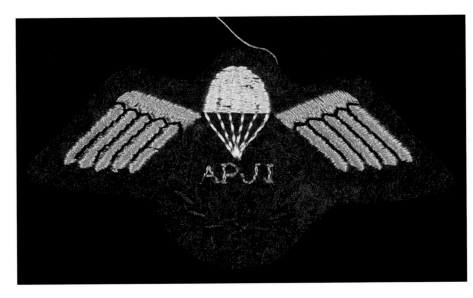

Badge of an assistant parachute jump instructor, the Parachute Regiment.

was redesignated the 51st and while their colleagues languished in German prisoner of war camps, the 'new' 51st distinguished itself at El Alamein and for a time in Italy, after which it returned to Britain, retrained and excelled yet again in France following D-Day. The 51st Highland Division was disbanded at the war's end, but revived as a territorial brigade in 1948 until 1967 from which period the distinctive 'HD' patch shown here dates.

However, perhaps no fabric badge is more distinctive than the winged dagger of the Special Air Service (SAS) beret badge, also shown here. The SAS has its origins in North Africa in 1941 when Capt David Stirling raised detachments of specialist raiding parties who, working closely with the Long Range Desert Group, caused havoc behind enemy lines with sabotage operations against German and Italian air fields and fuel dumps. The term 'Special Air Service' was chosen as part of a deception plan intended to convince the enemy that the British had increased their airborne assets in the region. The Regiment shot to fame in 1980 when it stormed the Iranian Embassy in

Badge of a qualified air despatch instructor, Royal Corps of Transport.

Fabric Special Air Service beret badge.

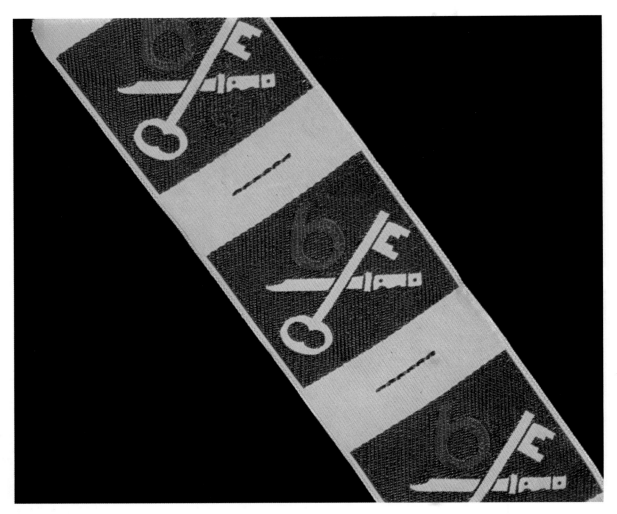

Post-Second World War 6th Infantry Brigade formation sign; the 5th Infantry Brigade also wore this emblem – a key crossing a bayonet.

London. During the Falklands campaign and during the more recent conflicts in the Gulf, the Regiment again distinguished itself. During the Gulf War of 1991, for example, it recreated some of the kinds of exploit for which it had been famous in the desert nearly fifty years before.

Mention of the SAS cloth badge shown in this book provides a good opportunity to talk about Special Forces insignia in general. While the clandestine nature of the work of these top secret units, covert intelligence gathering, sabotage and infiltration deep behind enemy lines, would suggest that the men of these units are better off without any identifiable insignia, human nature tells us that whatever unit a soldier joins – he expects to be able to wear its insignia. In my opinion the British regimental system works rather like the Football Association does – both organizations encourage a loyalty to individual teams (regiments) that to the outsider borders on the fanatical.

Today, although members of British Special Forces such as the Special Air Service and Special Boat Squadron (SBS), for example, are issued with insignia, there is an unwritten rule forbidding the publication of any personnel currently employed in such units. This goes some way to preventing an unnecessary risk

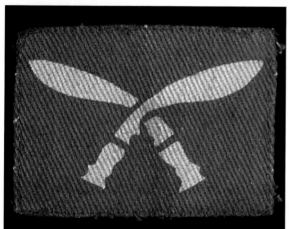

ABOVE: Army Signallers' badge.

LEFT: Formation sign of the 99th Gurkha Infantry Brigade featuring the kukri, the famous fighting knife of these Nepalese soldiers.

BELOW LEFT: Formation sign of the 63rd Gurkha Infantry Brigade.

BELOW: Post-war Guards Armoured Brigade flash (during the Second World War it did not feature any Roman numerals).

Post-Second World War 17th Indian Division formation sign. This was adopted by the 17th British Division serving during the Malayan emergency (the original sign was created in 1943 but was yellow on a khaki background).

ABOVE: Formation flash of the 2nd Army.

BELOW: United Nations embroidered badge as worn by British troops on peacekeeping duties.

to an individual soldier's life should he inadvertently be recognized via a press article.

The Sandys Defence White Paper of 1957 not only heralded the end of National Service in 1963 but axed over fifty major units, including thirty regiments. Two more rounds of reductions in 1972 and 1995 streamlined the Army still further. While the regimental system survives (just), it does mean that many famous units have bitten the dust.

For the collector, one result of all the cuts and reductions is the large number of available cloth and metal regimental shoulder titles belonging to units long gone. These will never be made again, and although some reproduction insignia can be purchased, the supply of original items is dwindling fast.

THE GENUINE ARTICLE: ORIGINAL OR REPRO?

Badge collectors have long suffered from the huge quantity of fake items on the market. We have seen that as early as the mid nineteenth century counterfeit items, in this case shako plates, were manufactured to fuel a demand from enthusiasts and relatives keen to celebrate the actions of British regiments in the Battle of Waterloo in June. The commemorative Waterloo emblems were produced without any subterfuge and were welcomed as useful mementoes of the Napoleonic Wars. So, not all reproduction insignia

are manufactured to deceive the purchaser into believing he has bought an authentic item.

There are a great many quite genuine – if that is not a contradiction in terms – reproduction ('repro') items on the market. These are generally manufactured to provide re-enactors and those educationalists involved in out-reach programmes for schoolchildren how soldiers used to live and what uniforms and insignia they wore. Additionally, before the processes governing the disposal of surplus government stock were tightened,

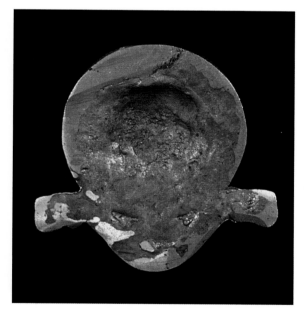

There are essentially two forms of re-strikes – reproduction badges – on the market. The first type are technically fakes. In this case an impression is taken from a genuine badge and a silicone or clay mould is manufactured into which a lead alloy or a similar low melting point metal is poured and a casting is made. The second (and, since the 1970s when genuine British Army moulding tools were unwittingly sold to dealers, now the more common) are replicas produced from authentic dies and often indistinguishable from the real thing. However, both methods generally fail to reproduce detail on the reverse of replica badges – as this Royal Scots Fusilier cap badge shows.

Although the manufacturer of this 8th Battalion Punjab Regiment badge clearly had access to the original manufacturing die, his use of cheap brass and the lack of clarity in the stamping clearly reveals this example to be a worthless re-strike.

Though of lower value than their metal compatriots, even cloth badges are subject to fakery. Badges of the Special Forces, such as this course-only trained parachutist emblem, belongs to the Parachute Regiment, a unit with such a caché that the market for their items is rarely diminished.

quantities of unissued badges and rank emblems were offloaded at auction to be snapped up by film and television costumiers. Many honest dealers sell repro items and mark them as such, making historic badges available to enthusiasts for a fraction of the price of the real thing. Finally, it must never be forgotten that a lot of veterans' associations provide their members with repro regimental badges, along with items such as ties, 'sweetheart' brooches and stationery. It is perfectly possible for these to be included in the sale of a veteran's possessions, bought by a dealer with all the provenance of association with an old soldier and consequently and innocently then be sold as real. Nevertheless, the collector, especially the novice, should be aware that, because of the increasing value of military insignia, there is money in fraudulently passing off a re-strike as an original item.

Spotting the Genuine Article

Fortunately, there are a number of ways to tell a genuine item from a fake. The first and simplest method if you want to avoid being ripped off is to use a faculty all of us can engage but many of us ignore – common sense. The adage that you get nothing for nothing is as true today as ever. Beware of 'bargain offers'. They seldom exist – certainly as far as badges are concerned. Authentic insignia that are seventy or eighty years old are going to cost money. Unless they are marked as repro, if you see regimental items for sale for knock-down prices they are probably fake. All dealers know the true values of badges and insignia and there are enough up-to-date collectors' guides to study, which either provide a price estimate for individual badges or at least give an indication of which types are the most expensive. So, study the bibliography for suggestions of reference books worth studying and ... do your research.

Ironically, although the current wealth of reference material is a boon to collectors, it has also enriched the counterfeiter too, providing accurate information, not only on what a badge looks like, but on how to detect fakes – these books can thus be used as guides to help

The too bright gold of this fake Control Commission Germany badge reveals it as another re-strike. The collector will also take note of the poor definition and especially the moulding flash evident around the edges of the CCG monogram. (The CCG was the umbrella organization that integrated civil engineers, policemen and other administrators who temporarily wore army uniforms and assisted with the redevelopment and government of the British sector of Germany in the immediate post-war years.)

the dishonest create realistic fakes. Nevertheless, these works will not simply give you an indication of values, they will also let you look at photographs of the real things. Notice how crisp genuine badges are; repro items are often second-generation castings, the original badge being used as the pattern from which a plaster or silicone mould is cast, and every time a copy is made the quality is reduced.

A badge's face is not the only place to investigate to determine whether the item is a re-strike. Often it is best judged by simply turning it over. The majority of badges are manufactured from sheet metals that have been pressed and then punched out so that all the detail is embedded in relief. Badges that have been reproduced by a limited-run casting process will often have flat, rather than concave backs. This is because when the molten metal has been poured into the mould its surface naturally dries flat.

Re-strikes

The issue of re-strikes and reproduction badges has been significantly complicated by the fact that since the 1970s many authentic dies and moulds have been legitimately acquired by dealers – I remind the reader of Nick Hall's story above about the West Midlands'-based dealer who purchased the dies of some of the long-gone British regiments.

Before the original manufacturing tools found their way into the supply chain, facsimiles were produced by using a variety of rather more amateurish techniques and the quality of the finished badges depended upon the skills of the forger, those who were the most conversant with moulding techniques and purchased the highest grades of alloy producing the most realistic looking badges. But the acquisition of the original dies meant that the forger – as opposed

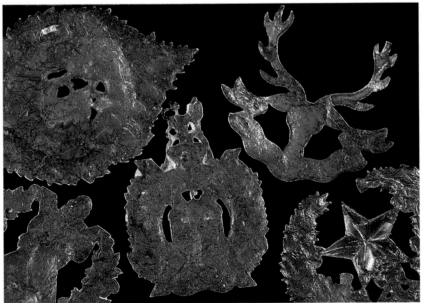

Often badges that might be supposed to be fake are actually manufacturers' samples intended for display and consequently produced with flattened or wax-filled backs to enable them to be more easily mounted. This assortment of Scottish badges includes those of the Argyll and Sutherland Highlanders, The King's Own Scottish Borderers, the Cameronians (Scottish Rifles) and the Seaforth Highlanders.

to the producer of legitimate items produced for the-atrical or re-enactment use – could achieve accurate impressions of the originals more easily.

However, as can be seen from the re-strikes shown here, the possession of the original tools will not guar-antee flawless reproduction, for without access to pro-fessional machinery those involved in reproducing original badges from authentic dies seldom achieve optimum mould pressure, with the result that much of the often low-grade alloy used seeps between the mould halves leaving a great deal of unattractive flash.

The other big give-away with re-strikes, again which can be seen from the examples shown, is that they are seldom produced in metals that look even close to the grades used by the original government suppliers. Usually they are far too bright, the alloy mix is also generally of inferior quality, with the result that the finished badges not only look the wrong colour but they also appear far lighter than they should.

Sand Casts

Sabre Sales's Nick Hall reminded me that some appar-ently fake badges were actually war-time sand casts that were made officially for regiments on service overseas.

> If a British regiment was stationed in Egypt, for exam-ple, they can't ring up one of the major badge manu-facturers back home and say they wanted some new badges. Not at all, in fact, they would take a badge down to the nearest bazaar where a tradesman would get some very fine quality sand. The badge would be dipped in the sand and a new one would be cast in the resulting impression – a "sand cast". Before the metal has solidified in the sand two metal plugs or a bar are stuck into the back. The result is that some regiments would have worn bazaar-made badges. Although, they were not renowned for their longevity, in the 1950s and the 1960s both India and Pakistan were two of the major sources of repro badges in the world.

Hall pointed out that during the Second World War badges manufactured in this way, while a unit was overseas, were to all intents and purposes 'official'. However, those produced by the same methods post-war were distinctly unofficial and produced only to satisfy a demand, often from old soldiers who had had to hand their badges in upon demobilization. Either way, as he said, serious badge collectors 'wouldn't really brook' such low-grade reproductions.

Cloth Badges

Metal badges are not the only insignia subject to reproduction, of course. Fabric items are also repro-duced, sometimes dishonestly. As with metal items, to distinguish real from fake cloth badges requires expe-rience – almost literally a 'nose' for the job, this is because one of the ways enthusiasts can determine the authenticity of an item is to smell it – the fibres of old material have a distinctive, musty aroma. Although the dishonest seller employs an armoury of techniques to age or distress an item, no amount of staining with weak tea can replace the smell of the genuine product. There are some rather more elaborate methods to employ when trying to determine right from wrong as far as cloth insignia are concerned. One is to attempt to tease out a strand of fabric from the edges of the badge (first get the owner's permission), when touched by a lit match synthetic fibres will shrink, forming a round blob that retreats from the heat, but cotton or woollen fibres from which most pre-1950 badges were made will simply burst into flame.

Some more hardcore enthusiasts employ methods such as ultraviolet (or 'black') light, which reveals poly-ester (synthetic) fibres by their shining, whereas natural fibres are inconspicuous because they do not reflect it.

Frustratingly, unless you can be sure that cloth insignia have been removed from an obviously origi-nal uniform it can be difficult to detect post-war fakes since the standards of manufacture are so high.

Enthusiasts must not forget, however, that the badges of some smaller units, generally of cloth, were locally made so that the quality of authentic items does vary considerably. Added to this is the fact men-tioned earlier by Hall that even regimental cap badges

were manufactured in theatre in Africa, the Middle East and India; to add another complication even some genuine badges may be poor reproductions.

The dramatic advances in computer-aided technology, allowing cutting, milling and die-stamping tools to be linked to mould etching or casting machines, have made the problems of re-strikes even more

LEFT: **Second World War 2nd Infantry Division formation sign featuring the crossed keys of the Archbishopric of York.**

BELOW: **Fabric beret badge of The Queen's Regiment (1970s).**

significant than ever before. This lack of concern about authenticity has now made it easier fo reproductions to be passed off as originals and high production standards mean that it is often hard to detect fakes. I cannot stress enough the need for enthusiasts, and especially novice collectors, to scrutinize genuine items in order to determine exactly how the real thing is supposed to look. Books are a good place to start, but a museum is the best place for the average collector to see the real thing. Some suggestions were listed earlier.

Demand fuels supply. If someone is prepared to part with hard-earned cash for an item that he has long desired and despite nagging doubts as to the object's provenance, then if a reasonable sum has been paid

The leaping gazelle of XIII Corps' formation sign.

Group 'A' tradesman, Guards Division.

Canadian Second World War Nova Scotia Highlanders' shoulder title.

and he is happy with the transaction, then fair enough; it is the excessive fleecing of the innocent novice that I want to avoid.

It might be a case of life following art, but there is one area of the repro market in which badges of dubious heritage – often quite poorly manufactured – are worth more than the real thing. The sector in question? Badges and regalia used in television programmes or in feature films, the province of the studio props department. If it can be proved that an item featured in a classic war film such as *The Bridge over the River Kwai* or *A Bridge Too Far*, it is often considered to have a far higher value than the authentic item it mimics; if it can be proved to have had an association with the film's stars, its value will soar even higher.

More Things to Watch For

A common feature of reproduction insignia sold as real is they have been artificially aged. This can be hard to detect, but the smell and patina of years gone by can never be accurately simulated. The other big cheat involves altering the location of the mounting lugs or the entire removal of such fittings so that they can be switched from one piece of headdress to another. Often the combination of two items that previously would never have been united creates an item of improbable reality, especially if it comes at a bargain price.

A note about the lugs, pins and fixtures of cap and collar badges – original items reveal a continuation of surface finish and tone that a badge with a recently soldered pin can never suggest. Do not let anyone trick you into believing that an example of remedial work on a badge or some other item was a 'field repair'. In their day badges and items of military equipment were low value, utilitarian pieces, when they broke or went missing they were if possible replaced from the quartermaster's stores. Alternatively, a few coins handed to a trader close to a unit's depot would deliver a replacement badge in time to avoid the RSM's wrath regarding the original's loss. Infantrymen certainly did not waste time mending insignia, so, if someone tries to sell you a badge with a blob of solder on it it has probably been done to deceive.

Some things to look out for: first, a change in the surface finish on a metal item suggesting that it is the marriage of two different pieces; evidence of solder, file marks and, worst of all, traces of adhesive.

Unless they are fresh from dark storage, period cloth items should exhibit some evidence of colour fading, items that have supposedly been worn in combat without any trace of stitch marks, holes or loose threads have clearly never been in battle. Lastly, but of no less importance, be aware of traces of a synthetic thread such as nylon in any British badge dating from or before the Second World War.

Nick Hall described the methods he uses to tell a real from a fake badge: 'The first way to avoid buying

Second World War King's crown embroidered regimental sergeant major's badge of rank worn on the lower sleeve of service dress.

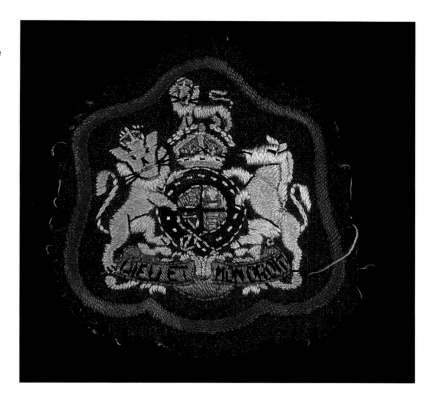

Post-Second World War Queen's crown embroidered regimental sergeant major's badge of rank worn on the lower sleeve of service dress.

Signals qualification emblems worn above rank insignia (chevrons) to denote attendance at, in this case, the Hythe Signals Wing.

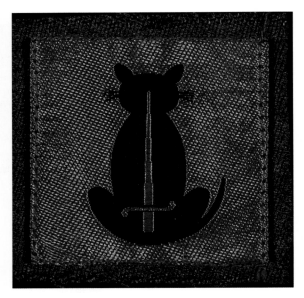

Second pattern 56th (London) Armoured Division (TA).

a facsimile is to honestly consider whether the price of the badge on offer is too good to be true. You can't get something of real value for a really cheap price. Therefore a knock-down bargain is probably fake. The second criterion I employ is to question the bona fides of the dealer. Is he or she someone you can trust? A reliable, well-known dealer will tell you exactly what something is and, if it is in anyway unusual or rare, then it will be priced accordingly.' The final method he uses depends on all the experience he has acquired down the years. It is a simple and pragmatic test: 'I pick a badge up in my hand and bounce it about. Is it too heavy? Is it too light?' The novice collector should be wary of employing a similar technique until he has handled as many badges as Hall.

CARING FOR YOUR COLLECTION: CONSERVATION AND DISPLAY

Regardless of how large or valuable your badge collection is, you want to be sure that the time and money invested is not wasted because of damage caused by poor storage or display. Army badges, like the soldiers who wore them, might be quite tough but they are not indestructible. Whether they are of metal manufacture or made from fabric, there are certain things that can be done to prevent further deterioration.

The writers Kipling and King made one important point about display: they advised collectors not to bother to arrange items for any kind of exhibition at home or to colleagues in a collectors' society, for example, until they were sure that the arrangement was comprehensive. You will waste a lot of time, they said, and create much unnecessary work in dismantling a display only to be forced to rearrange them for showing. But they did encourage even beginners to organize their finds. They recommended arranging badges on white card (or some material of another colour if it better suited the badges) and making holes through which mounting pins and lugs could be inserted and secured on the reverse with sticky tape or thread. These doyens of badge collectors recommended interleaving card sheets with corrugated cardboard to prevent damage to the badges. They also stressed how important it is not to have too many layers. The weight of hundreds of metal badges is not inconsiderable, too many will only result in the pins and securing lugs on the badges at the bottom bending or, even worse, snapping off altogether.

Collectors of cap badges lucky enough to have reunited them with their appropriate head-dress or who have bought them complete with the original hat or cap on which they were worn, such as this Argyll and Sutherland Highlanders' badge and glengarry, need to conserve the badge and the fabric. The white metal badge needs little care, but the glengarry would be prone to the attentions of moths if left unprotected. Bright sunlight will also cause the colour to fade, especially the rather fugitive red on the distinctive chequered dicing.

Moisture

Moisture is a big enemy to both cloth and metal. Fabrics will develop mould if they get wet and are not thoroughly dried, and metals will corrode.

If, for whatever reason, items in your possession, metal and fabric, get damp the first action is to make sure that they are dried. First, carefully unpack all the items and lay them out on a clean absorbent surface

such as sheets of kitchen towelling (if they are wrapped in tissue and this is damp, discard it). After some of the moisture has been absorbed, carefully lift the pieces off the kitchen towel, turn them over and place them the other way up on new towelling, discarding the used sheets. Allow the items plenty of time to dry naturally and make sure that they are placed where there is free circulation of air.

When all the badges are perfectly dry it is time to inspect them for damage. I use a toothbrush to remove any debris and corrosion, but obviously if too much deterioration has occurred on a badge its value will be greatly compromised, it might not even be worth keeping.

With a fabric item that might have developed a slight 'bloom' of mould it is possible to lift foreign matter from its surface by simply wrapping sticky tape – adhesive side outermost – around a finger and gently picking up any flecks of debris.

Staining is more difficult to remove. In general, it is inadvisable to attempt any drastic remedial action but sometimes the marking is so severe that an item is unfit for display or addition to a collection unless it is cleaned. In extreme cases I have used a proprietary stain remover of the kind that comes in a spray dispenser and is intended for use on garments before

ABOVE LEFT: **This Royal Essex Regiment cap badge reveals years of neglect and evidence of corrosion. Careful cleaning, as described in the text, is the only possible remedy. Often, however, once all the verdigris is removed the resultant pitting can reduce a badge's value enormously.**

LEFT: **Evident and typical damage shown on this Army Cyclist Corps shoulder title and shoulder grenade worn above the 'RF' on the epaulettes of fusiliers.**

they are put into a washing machine, and carefully applied this with a soft toothbrush to discoloured areas. Then the affected portion is carefully rinsed in warm water and the drying process resumed again. This is strictly a last resort, but it can be successful and I have removed ink stains and discoloration caused by damp packaging coming into contact with an item.

Badly corroded Second World War King's crown cap badge of the Royal Army Service Corps. Storage in damp or humid conditions will result in the rapid deterioration of brass badges.

Storage

Obviously prevention is better than cure and to avoid moisture damage from happening in the first place should be a priority of the collector. Even if you have to resort to storing badges in boxes and consigning them to cupboards or more remote storage, if they are packed with forethought there should not be a problem. Items should be carefully packed, with individual badges ideally wrapped in acid-free tissue paper and then separated from other pieces by layers of bubble wrap or quantities of expanded polystyrene chips. Sachets of desiccated silica gel will absorb any moisture that might penetrate the box. However, boxes that might conceivably get wet should be covered in plastic, but be careful that any water present

runs away from the boxes and that they are not left sitting in pools that might have collected.

One of my most useful tips for storing objects so that they will not suffer from the debilitating action of moisture sounds obvious but is often overlooked: do not transfer items from one extreme of temperature to another. For example, in winter loft spaces can be quite cold, especially if the spaces between joists have been properly insulated. Boxes sitting on the top of these will be at a much lower temperature than the rooms below. But, assuming that they contain metal badges and the boxes are opened in a centrally-heated house, repacked in the warm and immediately replaced in a chilly loft, condensation may develop on the items as they cool rapidly. This can happen in reverse: cold items will feel quite damp if they are hastily unwrapped in a much warmer environment. All this activity will encourage corrosion.

Humidity can be a problem for displayed as well as stored items. Badges exhibited behind glass in collectors' cabinets can suffer from the changes in temperature in our centrally-heated homes. Be careful that

Service dress sleeve patch designating a bandsman.

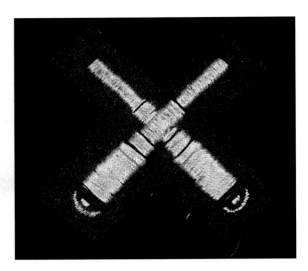

Sleeve emblem worn by Royal Artillery assistant instructors and qualified NCOs.

Another seemingly obvious thing to think about before you prepare items for display is to ensure that they can be easily removed or at least be dusted. Unless you install your prizes in a hermetically sealed, glass-fronted container, even the best cabinet will admit some dust. It is unavoidable, especially if you use a cabinet of the most typical sort where the entire front is hinged.

I have found the best way to dust badges on display is to use an air cleaner of the type used by photographers. It is designed to blow dust from lenses and to remove specks from inside cameras or from digital sensors, but it also makes it easy to remove dust from the recesses of badges; more stubborn debris can be removed with a brush.

cloth insignia displayed in such a way do not come into contact with the glass front of a cabinet; this material can transfer heat by convection and affect any materials with which it is in contact. Ideally, it is a good idea to permit some air flow around displayed objects, but it is important to ensure that moths and other predators cannot get inside cabinets.

Light

Light is another important consideration. Direct sunlight will cause cloth badges to fade, especially those where red or scarlet dominate in the design. Red is the most fugitive pigment, this is why red oil paint that will last is expensive and why red cars look good when new but less so in only a few years. Sunlight is also, of course, a source of heat, you would be amazed at how quickly the small space inside a display cabinet can heat up if it is subjected to sunlight. It is also important to avoid displaying items, especially those made from dyed fabrics, in a cabinet with internal lights: the atmosphere inside will soon become warm and, when the illumination is switched off at night, the cycle of temperature variation will begin again.

Cabinets

My own way of keeping badges safe, clean and accessible is to use the metal multi-drawer cabinets sold by stationery shops and business equipment suppliers and intended to keep A4 sheets of paper neatly to hand. I have found that by cutting a rectangle of foam plastic around 1 cm thick and placing it in the bottom of each draw and covered by black velvet or a similar material my badges can be safely stored and ready for immediate inspection. Another advantage of these cabinets is that they do not look like the kind of place in which one might store valuables, whereas some of the purpose-built cabinets manufactured for collectors do tend to suggest that their contents might be worth stealing.

There are many handsome compartmentalized display cases available. Manufactured from leatherette-covered chipboard or MDF and fitted with flock-covered trays or velvet liners, these units may be the perfect solution. Those with deeper pockets can opt for versions manufactured in oak or perhaps finished in a walnut or rosewood veneer. Often intended for wall hanging, these devices are equally suitable for placing in a drawer or on top of a shelf.

Some quality display cases are manufactured in the form of shallow trays, often pressed from a single

This badge belonging to the 3rd Battalion, the Monmouthshire Regiment reveals deposits that though harmless, lower the visual appeal of the badge. Careful cleaning using the processes described in this chapter is required.

piece of metal to ensure stability. Into these, flock-covered, compartmentalized, vacuum-formed inserts may be placed in which badges can be safely stored. Display cases of this type often feature glazed fronts that may be opened and secured with side struts, making it possible to rearrange the contents.

A much cheaper, but no less practical method of display and storage is to use an artist's display folio. Many of these come with transparent plastic pockets, available in a variety of sizes from A4 to the massive A0 format. These pockets may be used to display a wide range of items; it is especially easy to put cloth badges into them, but even metal insignia may be displayed. Individual badges simply have to be put inside separate plastic pouches and then two or three of these can be attached inside one A4 pocket, for example. Of course, a group of metal badges will reduce the available display space, especially when foam interleaving has been placed between the pockets to avoid any damage caused by metal pressing against metal.

Metal Discoloration

Metal items made of brass or bronze are also subject to natural discoloration. Both brass and bronze are alloys of copper, as are gunmetal, bell metal and nickel silver. Brass is an alloy containing about 70 per cent copper and 30 per cent zinc, bronze has a much higher copper content, about 90 per cent with 6 per cent tin and 4 per cent zinc.

It is perfectly natural for uncoated copper alloys to develop brownish or even blackish tarnishes. These are the result of non-corrosive oxidation and are nothing to worry about. On many historic items this patina testifies to the age of an object and is coveted by collectors. Sometimes this tarnish can accumulate quite thickly, but it is nothing to worry about and, on the contrary, it has the effect of preserving the base metal.

Generally, it is not a good idea to use abrasive cleaners to polish a badge, although serving soldiers were ordered to do so. However, every time a soldier

This Second World War vintage Royal Artillery cap badge displays the residue of years of polishing with Brasso; it is merely the patina of age.

polished a badge or some other brass accoutrement such as a belt buckle, he removed a quantity of metal. Similarly, every time a collector polishes a vintage badge he will be removing some surface detail.

However, if a bright green powder accumulates on a badge surface, and especially in cavities, this is an indication of active corrosion, often known as 'bronze disease'. This is to be avoided because, if it is left unchecked, it will result in pitting and the loss of more surface detail. This form of corrosion is caused by the presence of salts in the air or left on the badge because of inappropriate cleaning, especially in humid conditions. Dust and areas of surface dirt can actually trap moisture and encourage corrosion, so it is important to ensure that cavities especially are carefully brushed clean.

Cleaning

Mishandling can also cause significant damage to metal badges. Many vintage cap badges feature fine details that are easily bent or broken; details on the Buffs' cap badge mentioned earlier are particularly susceptible to damage through rough handling. Even gentle handling with bare hands can cause problems – our skin is rich with oils and can leave salt deposits that are capable of causing the corrosion of alloys, especially brass. Fingerprints can actually etch themselves into the surface of an old badge, so it is wise to wear linen gloves of the sort that can be purchased in photographic dealers when handling particularly valuable badges.

If a collector is forced to resort to cleaning a badge – perhaps it has been kept in a box full of old and dirty

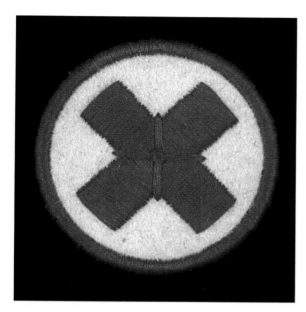

Badge of the Royal Army Medical Corps, medical orderly.

objects – then it is possible to do so with some simple materials, including water. Most conservationists recommend using a solution of 3 per cent soap mixed with distilled water. If the badge has traces of grease or paint it is permissible to use mineral oil to wipe off such marks before washing in the soap solution. It is even possible to use a 10 per cent solution of Calgon to remove limescale deposits that may have found their way on to a badge surface.

After these treatments have been used, the items should be given a final rinse in distilled water. To finish off, the badges should be dried by using kitchen towels and, once all traces of moisture have been removed, given a final inspection before being stored, ideally in a container that includes some silica gel to absorb any remaining traces of moisture. But I must stress that cleaning a badge should be attempted only if the item is in a really poor shape and encrusted with grease, dirt or paint. In general, it is wiser to leave it in its original condition.

I asked Nick Hall what he thought was the best way to protect and display a badge collection. 'Well, almost the most important consideration regarding metal badges is to be aware of their appeal to thieves',

he stressed. 'Hanging them up all around a room isn't such a good idea. Badges are the one thing thieves always go for. Another consideration in modern homes is humidity – the fluctuation of which does nothing but harm to metal badges. I would recommend that you get a lockable cabinet and store them in this. There are differing schools of thought about whether they should be cleaned for display. One says never clean them at all. If you do, you are removing the patina of age. And, of course you can't clean an anodized badge, a Staybrite badge. It is what it is, there's nothing you can do about it, other than a gentle rub with a specialist cloth. I don't think badges should be cleaned. With helmet plates, for example, you are rubbing away the lovely gilding if you do. Brasso is extremely abrasive – you can use it to clean motor-bike engines …'.

I asked him about the importance of condition to the collector. 'Yes. Condition is very important. A very dear friend of mine, Sam Hill, also collected badges. He was a very great soldier during the Second World War, working with the reconnaissance unit of The King's Royal Rifle Corps, with F/M Lord Bramall as his platoon commander at that time. He had a thing about putting badges on boards. Being a welder by trade, he was in the habit of cutting the backs off and then screwing on the most awful lugs to the backs of each badge. When Sam Hill died I arranged for all his badges to be sold. I'm told that when the chap who bought them inspected his purchase, he burst into tears because he had never seen so much damage. For years, I had told Sam "Don't do that", but he insisted on doing it because it suited him.'

Hall reminded me of how happy Rifleman Hill of The King's Royal Rifle Corps was about the plastic badges employed during the war to save precious metal that was better used for the manufacture of munitions. The KRCC's metal cap badge was finished in black and consequently soldiers were forever having to touch them up with paint as the rigours of Army life took their toll on their original finish. The new black Bakelite badges were warmly received by the rank and file – they never needed a lick of paint.

As is probably the case with most collectors, some of the badges in my collection have damaged lugs

The value of this Durham Light Infantry Second World War King's crown economy Bakelite cap badge has been drastically reduced by the damage to the lugs on its back. Although extremely rare, the fixings of the metal lugs on the reverse of these badges are prone to damage – often caused by poor storage. Collectors of such items should always check the integrity of any metal fastenings – broken lugs are almost impossible to repair.

and pins, obviously reducing their value. Nick told me that there were firms that specialize in repairing badges, but that it was a tricky business since, if too much heat was applied when soldering or annealing a badge's fittings, the face and impression of the badge itself could be inadvertently damaged. 'It's not something you want to do yourself,' he said, 'you can quite easily melt the badge.'

So, prevention is better than cure and to ensure that lugs, pins and other attachments are not broken nor bent, the collector is advised to check how his precious badges are stored and, if it is evident that too much weight is bearing down on the badges at the bottom of a box for example, I would recommend their immediate repacking and the addition of foam rubber or bubble wrap layers to relieve the pressure.

BUYING AND SELLING: ONLINE, MILITARY FAIRS AND AUCTIONS

At the beginning of the twenty-first century it is a happy coincidence that, although the supply of badges seems to be evaporating, with many provincial junk shops and local antique dealers having disappeared and being replaced by so-called 'antique centres' or collectors' markets, there is a new shop window through which perhaps the widest ever selection of badges may be seen: the internet.

Online

Just as it was becoming increasingly difficult to find or purchase a bargain, even once inexpensive charity shops are aware of the true value of bygones and are now pricing 'collectables', even second-hand books accordingly, enthusiasts now have the opportunity to shop at an international market and bid for items at knock-down prices. The biggest and most successful online auction business is eBay, although there are an increasing number of specialist collectors' communities where items can be bought and sold, not simply discussed or exhibited. I can talk with some authority since

Slip-on rank insignia for infantry staff sergeant.

From the 1960s: British infantryman's rank insignia (tapes) for a staff sergeant wearing the thick, KF (khaki flannel) shirt-sleeve order.

I established one of them, www.collectingfriends.com. Nevertheless, most readers are likely to make eBay their first port of call when searching for that missing badge or perhaps intending to sell some unneeded spares, eBay is excellent and I use it a great deal.

However, to get the most out of it, it is worth bearing in mind some simple rules. What follows is intended to maximize your online experience, helping you to achieve the best prices for items posted for sale and, conversely, explaining how to purchase for the lowest price.

The index of categories on eBay is vast. However, three categories are of particular use to the badge collector:

Collectables>Militaria>World War II (1939–1945)

Collectables>Militaria>Other Militaria

Militaria in books, Comics & Magazines>Non-Fiction Books>Military/War

Badges and other items of regalia may also be located in:

Clothes, shoes and accessories>Vintage clothing and accessories and their various male or female and period subsets

As with all auctions, an item is automatically won by the highest bid. Fortunately, if you see something you

Although woefully unprepared for the public's response to its appeal for volunteers to join a new volunteer defence force, the government could at least be sure that morale was high. The Local Defence Volunteers and its successor the Home Guard enabled those too old or young for military service and key workers in reserved occupations to help in Britain's war effort.

want and are prepared to bid higher than the current price being offered, you do not necessarily have to spend too much. Bids on eBay increase incrementally, so even if you fancy an item with a current price of, say £50 and enter a maximum bid limit of £70, you might be lucky enough to secure the object you covet for only a few pounds more than the current top price. It all depends on how high others have set their limits, and it also depends on how long the auction has left to run. If it is a seven-day auction (the most common period) and it has only hours left to run you might be lucky. On the other hand, if you enter a maximum limit close to the current price at an earlier stage, do not be surprised if you are outbid nearer the

auction's end. As with all auctions, timing your bid is the key to success. One pf the fascinating things about eBay, for example, is watching the frenzy of bidding activity moments before a sale ends.

Similarly, when you are selling an item you must not be despondent if little seems to be happening during the first few days your sale items are on offer. Veteran eBayers hold back until the last minute and do not want to reveal their hands too early. After all, many early bids will only push the final price upwards and everyone wants to buy things for the best, that is, cheapest price.

If you do want sell an item on eBay the best indication of how well it might perform is to monitor the 'watchers'. These are people who have effectively 'bookmarked' your items and are keeping an eye on its price as the sale progresses. Sellers can see just how many people are watching items, other than seeing

ABOVE: **This Second World War National War Savings poster gives a pretty good idea of the amount of kit carried by the 'Poor Bloody Infantry'.**

RIGHT: **Published in 1942, this pocket guide to the badges of the entire regular and volunteer forces was a boon to schoolboy badge collectors.**

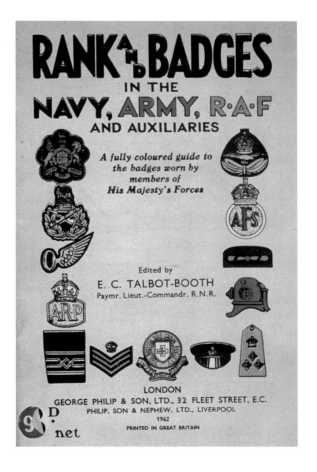

the bid prices rise; buyers have no idea how much interest your sale is generating. In my experience, it is not unusual to see an item achieve only one or two bids well into an auction, but by seeing how many potential bidders are watching your items you can gauge its popularity and likely success. I have sold items that have received no bids but have attracted many watchers and have been confident that, as the auction approaches its climax, my items will do well. I have seldom been disappointed. In the same way that timing your bid is important when attempting to buy an item, timing the end of your sale is equally crucial.

Like many other similar sites, eBay operates 24/7 and has a truly global reach. Therefore, because of the

world's time zones, someone, somewhere is looking at an item, regardless of whether you are tucked up in bed. However, assuming that you live in the United Kingdom and that you want to mange your sales as efficiently as possible and not have to set your alarm clock for the early hours to see how much your precious King's crown RA cap badge achieved when the auction closed, you will probably opt to start and finish your sale when you can most conveniently use your computer.

There are also other things to consider, not just reaching the biggest audience. In my experience, partners are not too keen to discover that either their evening out has been brought to an early end because

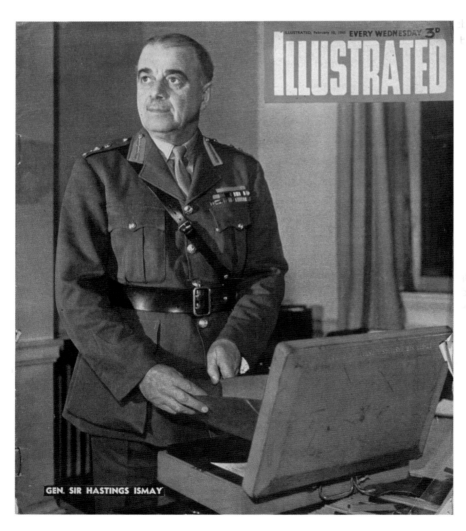

Gen Sir Hastings Ismay in the uniform of the supreme British staff officer of 1940.

you need to get online, or, worst of all, cancelled because you are watching a sale that is soon to close. Therefore, for a happy personal life, it makes sense to reach agreement with your family about when you should spend time online.

There are several views regarding the best time to start and to finish a sale, all having been developed as the result of hands-on experience. However, I think there are a few sensible things to bear in mind. I have found Saturday to be the best day to start and, consequently, allow a sale to end. However, not just at any time of the day, given that the majority of us have some obligations on a Saturday during the day and in the evening, I have found the time slot between 5.00 and 7.30p.m. to be the most satisfactory. I find Sunday to be less so; as regards weekdays I prefer Tuesday, Wednesday and Thursday at some time between 8.00 and 10.00p.m.

In my experience I have found that individuals from abroad, especially the United States, Australia and Japan, purchase the majority of my items of militaria. This is perhaps not surprising, for although it is still relatively easy for someone in Britain to find a Home Guard brassard, they are very scarce in the USA. But Europeans too are also very interested in British militaria and there seems to be a thriving collectors' base, especially for Home Front items, in France, Holland, Germany and Scandinavia.

The final key to achieving success when you sell an item online is to prepare its listing correctly. This involves making your description as accurate as possible, pointing out any defects or blemishes up front, since eBay thrives on trust. It has a self-regulatory mechanism known as 'Feedback' where buyers and sellers can rate individual transactions. This is a powerful tool; if you have disappointed a buyer for a variety of reasons, perhaps your badge was inaccurately described or so poorly packed that it arrived damaged, you will attract 'Negative feedback'. This kind of electronic bad karma must be avoided, it signals to other potential purchasers that you are untrustworthy and it is a devil to escape from.

Inaccurate listing is not the only potential deterrent to a successful sale, a poor photograph of your prize does equally little to inspire a purchaser. Digital

In arduis fidelis ('Faithful in adversity'), motto of the **Royal Army Medical Corps.**

cameras providing the resolution required to display even quite a large image on a computer screen (which is only 72dpi) are now relatively cheap; I use a 4 megapixel compact camera and it is fine. At the time of writing the capacity of similar cameras has doubled and prices continue to drop.

One advantage of the way many digital cameras work is their ability to focus closer than the lenses of cheap film cameras could. This is a result of a digital camera's ability to combine both optical resolution (what it sees through the glass of its lens) with digital extrapolation, enlarging the image recorded on the sensor. Consequently many reasonably priced digital cameras are capable of focusing close enough even to get acceptable images of badges.

Lighting is important, one sees too many online images ruined because they were lit by flash being situated immediately above the camera's optics. This harsh light has the effect of both bleaching out colour and flattening the subject. It will also cast a harsh shadow behind the badge. Therefore I would recommend investing in a tripod and using natural light if it is at all possible. Most modern digital cameras include a facility enabling the user to turn off the in-built flash, and the modelling provided from natural light will make your object look more attractive. But try to avoid harsh sunlight; in my experience overcast days, provided with what professional photographers call 'God's tracing paper', an overall layer of thin cloud that has the affect of diffusing the light, work best.

Military Fairs

But even if you are not looking to buy or sell online, it is a good place for research, showing you not only what an object looks like but also what its likely current value might be.

For those collectors without computer access or those unprepared for the potential risks (there are not many) of dealing with remote and unknown buyers and sellers or simply for those people who just like to shake hands on a deal, there are alternatives. I have mentioned specialist dealers earlier and I have also bemoaned the disappearance of the traditional junk shops and untidy collectors' grottos of my youth, but some military fairs still exist.

Perhaps the biggest and best militaria event held annually in the United Kingdom is the huge War and Peace Show held over four days in July at The Hop Farm Country Park, Paddock Wood in Kent. Though primarily a showcase for classic military vehicles and their dedicated owners (it was originally established by the Kent-based, Invicta Military Vehicle Preservation Society), together with around a thousand assorted tanks, trucks and vintage vehicles from around the world such as the German *Schwimmwagen* amphibious car and the American M3 half-track, supported by hundreds of re-enactors in period uniforms, this show features dozens of stands selling everything from books to badges.

Located relatively close to The War and Peace Show is Military Odyssey, situated at the Kent County Showground at Detling. Billed as the country's largest multi-period living history event, it also claims to be the biggest militaria event of its kind in the world. It has become a Mecca for enthusiasts over the August Bank Holiday weekend.

Arms and Armour UK is another well-known organizer of specialist militaria fairs, holding their first one in 1969. Currently they hold four Bedford Militaria Fairs each year, specializing in everything from swords and armour to aviation collectables, but especially badges and medals.

Another busy show is The Great Malvern International Military Convention, held on a regular basis at the Three Counties Showground in Worcestershire. Again, this show is a veritable militaria jamboree – all kinds of military items may be found there, with Army badges ranking prominently. Yet another well known fair is organized by HandS Militaria Fairs, who alternate

Embroidered University of London Officer Training Corps shoulder title.

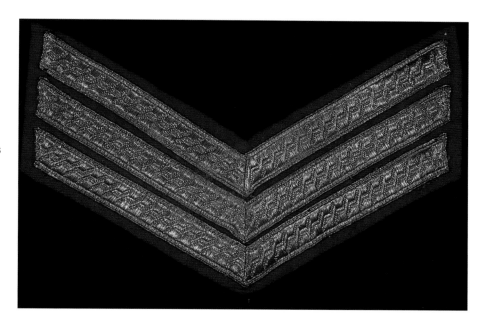

British Army sergeant's stripes as worn on the mess jacket.

Sunday shows between the Maltings in Farnham, Surrey and Cheshunt's Wolsey Hall in Hertfordshire. Together with World War Books, HandS Military Fairs have recently started a new fair called The Military Collectors Fair at Middle Wallop, Hampshire; at the time of writing the show was still to come, but I am sure it will be worth a visit. The Museum of Army Flying is close by.

Although specializing in quality arms and armour, the stands at The London Antique Arms Fair held in the Ibis Hotel in London's Earl's Court every April and September is another event worthy of a visit by the dedicated badge collector.

Although no longer held, I can't mention militaria fairs without reminiscing about the famous Warnham War Museum military collectables fairs held on this fascinating site in West Sussex on Sundays during the 1980s and early 1990s. The museum is long gone as, sadly, is the event's founder, the late Joe Lyndhurst.

Born in 1924, Joe was one of the pioneering militaria collectors in Britain. He was also especially significant in the development of the classic military vehicle hobby in this country. However, Joe is perhaps best known for his famous Warnham War Museum and, of course, for writing that most valuable resource of militaria collectors, *Military Collectables*, published by Salamander books in 1983 (still a great reference for badge collectors).

Gatherings at Warnham War Museum soon acquired near-legendary status amongst enthusiasts. The site began to host monthly militaria sales and auctions. The aforementioned Nick Hall, of Sabre Sales fame, was a regular stallholder at Warnham. The author has fond memories of sharing a cuppa with Nick and his then much younger sidekick Richard Ingram. Happy days…

Sadly, the collections outgrew even the substantial premises at Warnham and Joe was forced to sell. Following illness, Joe died in 2000. Fittingly, however, at the War & Peace show in 2005, Joe was awarded *After the Battle* magazine's 'Bart Vanderveen Challenge Shield' for his activities at Warnham and towards his activities in the classic military vehicle hobby in general.

Auctions

Buying at one of the many traditional auction houses is perhaps the last area to consider, although there are many auctioning badges and regalia. Probably foremost among them are Wallis and Wallis, opened in Lewes shortly after the Second World War by the late Maj J.P.S. Wallis. The business was initially involved in property and estate management, but, following the successful sale of a quantity of antique arms from a large country house, it was clear that there was a demand for items such as weapons, uniforms, armour and badges and medals. The company have never looked back and their elegant Edwardian premises at the heart of Lewes have long been an attraction for badge enthusiasts.

The military auctioneers and valuers Bosleys have been mentioned before, but they should be included high on the list of recommended specialist auction houses. Formed by the partnership of Stephen and Sally Bosley, each year this company holds four regular sales in its Thameside Georgian premises, attracting collectors from all over the globe. At the time of writing, their web site shows the prices reached at an auction of badges in January 2007. I think that they are worthy of inclusion here as they show collectors and enthusiasts what these items may be worth. For example, a pair of die-stamped brass RFC wings (NCO) realized nearly £200; an RAOC King's crown anodized cap badge nearly £500; a 22nd Dragoon's Second World War NCO's bimetal arm badge sold for £440; a Royal Devon Yeomanry Artillery anodized cap

badge sold for £198; a Second World War plastic Highland Regiment Glengarry badge achieved £110; a Connaught Rangers' silver-plated cap badge (1902–22) sold for £100 and a Shanghai Fire Brigade enamelled cap badge sold for a staggering £880.

For those collectors unable to visit Bosleys' premises the company also holds regular postal auctions. Each of these sales includes about 650 lots of badges and insignia spanning the armies of the British Empire.

Other specialist auctioneers include Sworders of Sudbury in Suffolk; London's Morton and Eden; Thomson Roddick and Medcalf based in Carlisle and Germany's Hermann Historica.

All the really famous international auctioneers (Sothebys, Christies and Bonhams) also feature regular militaria sales and it is worthwhile contacting them or looking at their web sites and asking to be put on their mailing list for advance notice of sales featuring badges.

I am sure that you will have no trouble in finding reliable sources from which to purchase genuine badges. Probably your biggest problem will be knowing when to stop – be warned as Kipling and King said, badge collecting is a disease.

BIBLIOGRAPHY

Books

Chandler, David and Bennett, Ian, *The Oxford Illustrated History of the British Army* (Oxford University Press)

Churchill, Colin and Westlake, Ray, *British Army Collar Badges, 1881 to the Present* (Arms & Armour Press)

Cook, H.C.B., *The Battle Honours of the British and Indian Armies 1662–1982* (Leo Cooper)

Davis, Brian L., *British Army Cloth Insignia, 1940 to the Present* (Arms & Armour Press)

Davis, Brian L., *German Army Uniforms and Insignia 1939–45* (Arms & Armour Press)

Gould, Robert W., *British Campaign Medals: Waterloo to the Falklands* (Arms & Armour Press)

Griffin, P.D., *Encyclopedia of Modern British Army Regiments* (Sutton Publishing)

Hodges, Lt Col Robin, *British Army Badges* (Lt Col & Mrs Robin Hodges)

Kipling, Arthur L. and King, Hugh L., *Head-Dress Badges of the British Army* (2 vols) (K+K)

May, W.E., Carmen, W.Y. and Tanner, Jon, *Badges and Insignia of the British Armed Services* (A. & C. Black)

Ripley, Howard, *Buttons of the British Army 1855–1970* (Arms & Armour Press)

Shortt, James G., *Special Forces Insignia British and Commonwealth Forces* (Arms & Armour Press)

Wilkinson, F., *Badges of the British Army 1820 to the Present* (Arms & Armour Press)

Wilkinson, F.J., *Badges and Emblems of the British Forces 1940* (Greenhill Books)

Specialist Magazines

The Armourer Militaria Magazine (Beaumont Publishing)
Classic Military Vehicle (Kelsey Publishing Group)
Medal News (Token Publishing)
Military Illustrated (Publishing News)
Skirmish: The Re-enactment Magazine (Dragoon Publishing)

INDEX